The Institute of Chartered Financial Analysts
Continuing Education Series

International Equity Investing

New York, New York
March 27, 1984

Edited by
James R. Vertin, CFA

Gary L. Bergstrom
Robert J. Boyd
Michael W. R. Dobson
David P. Feldman
David I. Fisher
William P. Marshall

Jeremy D. Paulson-Ellis
Ivan A. Pictet
Rodger F. Smith
Jan Twardowski
Karl R. Van Horn

Sponsored by
The Institute of Chartered
Financial Analysts

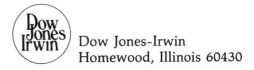
Dow Jones-Irwin
Homewood, Illinois 60430

© The Institute of Chartered Financial Analysts, 1984

This publication is designed to provide accurate and
authoritative information in regard to the subject matter
covered. It is sold with the understanding that the
publisher is not engaged in rendering legal, accounting, or
other professional service. If legal advice or other expert
assistance is required, the services of a competent
professional person should be sought.

*From a Declaration of Principles jointly adopted by a Committee
of the American Bar Association and a Committee of Publishers.*

ISBN 0-87094-649-8

Library of Congress Catalog Card No. 84–72415

Printed in the United States of America

4 5 6 7 8 9 0 K 1 0 9 8 7

Table of Contents

Foreword

Darwin M. Bayston, CFA
Vice President, Continuing Education

Unique opportunities exist in the field of international investments. Billions of dollars are invested annually in foreign equity markets by an increasing number of investment managers. The market value of U.S. equities represents only about 50 percent of the equity market value of all nations in the free world. Foreign markets, therefore, offer opportunities for increasing investment returns and/or reducing portfolio risk.

Although investing internationally offers possibilities for risk-return benefits, managers face many challenges in the investment processes of foreign markets. The accountability of assets within countries, fundamental economic differences, exchange rate factors, and varying standards of disclosure require an understanding of the complexities of investing in international securities.

This publication is the proceedings of a one-day seminar, "International Equity Investing", held on March 27, 1984 in New York, which explored the many important aspects of investing in international equity markets.

The Institute extends its appreciation to the seminar speakers: Gary L. Bergstrom, president, Acadian Financial Research, Inc.; Robert J. Boyd, group managing director, G.T. Capital Management; Michael W. R. Dobson, director, Morgan Grenfell Investment Services; David P. Feldman, assistant treasurer, American Telephone & Telegraph; David I. Fisher, president, Capital Research Company; William P. Marshall, vice president, GTE Investment Management Corp.; Jeremy D. Paulson-Ellis, director, Vickers da Costa; Ivan A. Pictet, partner, Pictet & Cie; Jan Twardowski, senior vice president, Frank Russell International; and Karl R. Van Horn, chairman, American Express Asset Management. A special thanks is extended to Rodger F. Smith, executive vice president, Greenwich Research Associates, who provided valuable guidance to the development of the program and served as moderator. Thanks is also extended to James R. Vertin, CFA, chairman of the Council on Continuing Education, the editor of this publication, and Cathryn E. Kittell, assistant vice president, Continuing Education. Each of them made a significant contribution to the program and to this publication.

Biographies of Speakers

Gary L. Bergstrom is president and chief investment officer of Acadian Financial Research, Inc., which specializes in financial and investment management services and worldwide asset management. Previously, Dr. Bergstrom was vice president of Putnam International Advisory Company, S.A. Dr. Bergstrom received his B.S. and M.S. from Purdue University and Ph.D. from Massachusetts Institute of Technology's Sloan School of Management.

Robert J. Boyd is group managing director and chairman of the Executive and International Investment Committees at G. T. Capital Management, Inc. which manages portfolios for clients from all over the world, including the United Kingdom, Middle East, France, Canada, and the United States. Previously, Mr. Boyd was an investment analyst with Henderson Administration. Mr. Boyd graduated from Oxford University.

Michael W. R. Dobson is a director of Morgan Grenfell Investment Services, responsible for managing ERISA accounts and coordinating European Research. Mr. Dobson began his career with Morgan Grenfell in Research and Fund Management. Mr. Dobson holds an M.A. from Cambridge University.

David P. Feldman is corporate vice president—Investment Management of American Telephone and Telegraph Company, responsible for the investment management of AT&T pension funds and savings plans. Mr. Feldman began his career with the Bell System and has served as director of Banking Relations and assistant treasurer. Mr. Feldman earned his B.S. from Purdue University and M.B.A from Illinois Institute of Technology.

David I. Fisher is president of Capital Research Company and director of The Capital Group, Inc. and is responsible for international activities. Previously, Mr. Fisher was second vice president and financial analyst for Smith Barney, Harris Upham and Co. Mr. Fisher earned a B.A. at the University of California and M.B.A at the University of Missouri Graduate School of Business Administration. .

William P. Marshall is vice president for Research and Strategies at GTE Investment Management Corporation, responsible for administering GTE's pension fund and other worldwide financial investments. Prior to joining GTE, Mr. Marshall was a security analyst with Fidelity Union Trust Company. Mr. Marshall received his B.S.B.A. from Babson College and M.B.A from Seton Hall University. Mr. Marshall also serves as chairman of the Financial Advisory Committee, District 2, U.S. Power Squadrons.

Jeremy D. Paulson-Ellis is director of Vickers da Costa, responsible for international developments, including the Far East and United States. Mr. Paulson-Ellis began his career with Vickers da Costa working with European and Japanese securities. Mr. Paulson-Ellis was educated at Sherborne School and attended university in France.

Ivan A. Pictet is a partner of Pictet and Company, the largest private Swiss bank. Mr. Pictet worked for Citibank, U.S. Trust and several U.S. brokerage firms before returning to Switzerland to join Pictet and Company as the fifth generation family partner. Mr. Pictet received his Baccalaureate Degree from the College de Geneve and M.B.A. from the School for Business Administration of St. Gallen.

Rodger F. Smith is executive vice president of Greenwich Research Associates, responsible for research and consulting programs in investment management. Previously, Mr. Smith was vice president of Investments for Allis-Chalmers Corporation. Mr. Smith earned both his B.S. and M.B.A. at the University of Wisconsin.

Jan Twardowski is senior vice president of Frank Russell International, the International Division of the Frank Russell Company. Previously, Mr. Twardowski was senior vice president at Wellington Management Company and the Vanguard Group. Mr. Twardowski received his B.S. from Princeton University and M.B.A. from The Wharton School of the University of Pennsylvania.

Karl R. Van Horn is chairman and chief executive officer of American Express Asset Management Holdings. Previously, Mr. Van Horn was Vice President and Head of International Investments with Morgan Guaranty Trust Company. Mr. Van Horn received his B.S. from Yale University and Masters Degrees from Cambridge University and Johns Hopkins University.

James R. Vertin, CFA is principal of Alpine Counselors. He recently concluded a career of thirty years with Wells Fargo Bank, involving management of Wells Fargo Investment Advisors. Mr. Vertin is a former president (1981–82) and trustee and is currently chairman of the Council on Continuing Education of the Institute of Chartered Financial Analysts. He is a former director of the Financial Analysts Federation and a current officer and trustee of the Financial Analysts Research Foundation. Mr. Vertin has authored numerous articles on pension and investment topics, including a chapter in the book *Managing Investment Portfolios: A Dynamic Process.* He received his M.B.A. from Stanford University.

Overview of the Seminar

James R. Vertin, CFA

The Institute of Chartered Financial Analysts, through its Continuing Education Program, has once again been pleased to present a seminar on a timely topic of importance to members and to the broad practitioner community. The subject, International Equity Investing, is an activity growing in scope and significance at a rapid pace. Our Moderator, Rodger F. Smith, executive vice president, Greenwich Research Associates was, with Darwin M. Bayston, CFA, director of the Institute's Continuing Education Program, the primary organizer of the seminar's content and personalities; he did a superb job of taking us through the day's events, from opening remarks to the closing Question and Answer session. These resultant Proceedings are presented in the hope that they will make a contribution to the reader's understanding of this global elaboration of the basic domestic investment management model with which we are so much more familiar.

Until the middle 1970s, it was a rare investment textbook that devoted any space at all to either the rationale for, or the pros and cons of, international investing. Indeed, even now most text writers continue to ignore this subject area or give it only a paragraph or two of very general comments.[1] As with the matter of real estate as an investment asset, the very valuable characteristics possessed by international securities and portfolios have been largely ignored by the U.S. business education and investment management communities until quite recently.

For the vast majority of American investors and investment managers, investing abroad has always had a certain mystery about it, not to mention at least a modicum of skepticism and even vague distrust. Until very recent years, and then only after some prominent firms led the way and made it "look like an OK thing to do," "foreign stocks" were not seen as proper for use on our own initiative as managers. Nor was it all that long ago that "foreign bonds" meant World

Bank issues or Canadians with governmental backing and principal and interest payable in U.S. dollars. Moreover, "foreign" was a word often used with condescension vis-à-vis U.S. investing.

Now, this may all be changing. As we see from our reading of these Proceedings, international investing is becoming an important new discipline for many U.S. investment management firms, at least in the pension area. For the few pioneers, like Capital Research, that have been investing abroad for many years, this development is no big thing. For the great majority of us, however, a conscious choice may soon be required as to whether or not we are going to enter this business in a serious way and, if so, by what means and to what degree. From experience, those familiar with the dimensions of that choice know that it is not an easy one to make; in fact, it is one with far-reaching implications and consequences.

It is particularly interesting to note that the "modern era" for international investing began only in 1974 with the arrival of ERISA and its much-enlarged definitions of prudence and diversification and its emphasis on the total portfolio as the appropriate context in which to evaluate risk and return. Even so, it was not until Morgan Guaranty put a portion of its pension clients' monies into a commingled fund for international investment exposure in 1974 that the mainstream management community had a role model with which to identify. To me, the significance of Morgan's action lies not so much in creating and making available a new vehicle through which to obtain overseas investment exposure but, rather, in the fact that *they put the monies into the fund on their own initiative*, utilizing their discretionary management authority to do so. Until then, even management organizations routinely offering investment abroad as part of their service packages tended to require that investors/clients come to them with a specific request to which they could respond. In a sense, Morgan's action "legitimatized" the notion of international investment by U.S. fiduciaries and lifted it out of its former narrow, almost covert, niche.

What's in it for the investor putting equity

---

[1] Exceptions to this rule include, by way of limited example, recent texts by James L. Farrell, Jr., Frank K. Reilly, and William F. Sharpe, which include reasonably complete discussions of the subject and its fundamentals.

money abroad? Improved diversification, surely —or so the theory says—relative to an all-U.S. portfolio, and—perhaps—improved returns as well. That combination is the driving force: at least the same level of return, and maybe a bit more, at a lower level of overall portfolio risk. But, what about currency fluctuations and political risks? How does one know how much to allocate and where to put it? What approaches have been found to work, what processes are required, and who makes which decisions? What does the performance record show, and how are results measured. What about differences in accounting, market illiquidity, and lack of data bases?

Those, and many other appropriate and helpful questions are what this seminar was about. Following Rodger Smith's stimulating and fact-filled introduction of the subject, Gary Bergstrom—from the practitioner's side—and Bill Marshall—from the plan sponsor's side—provide us with the theory, the practice, and the experience of the manager and the sponsor with money invested abroad. Then, Dave Feldman takes us step by deliberate step through one company's decision to start an international investment program, into the setting of objectives and the hiring of managers and, finally, into the implementation itself in a fascinating case study with a $1 billion outcome. Next, Jan Twardowski illuminates the monitoring and measurement dimensions of international portfolios and relates this to what we are familiar with in performance measurement terms for accounts invested domestically.

Switching the focus, Dave Fisher and Karl Van Horn take us into the worlds of the international security analyst and the analytical organization, exploring many of the essential aspects of the informational input side of the international investment coin. Both men speak with conviction and each provides some important insights on practice as it is and as it will change in the period ahead. They are followed by four international investment professionals, each with a specific geographic discussion assignment: Ivan Pictet on Continental Europe; Michael W. R. (Mike) Dobson on the United Kingdom and Scandinavia; Jeremy D. Paulson-Ellis on Australia, Singapore, and Malaysia, the "resource countries"; and Robert J. (Bertie) Boyd on Japan. They not only cover their assignments in depth and from personal knowledge, but each also imparts a flavor of the manager's role and adds a bit of personal philosophy along the way. At intervals, question and answer sessions occur, led with perceptive skill by Rodger Smith, who draws new meaning from some of the material presented and often elaborates it into broadened insights that aid our understanding.

This was an exciting, provocative, and thoroughly enjoyable event. The Trustees of the Institute join me in hoping that you find these Proceedings to be a valuable resource for keeping current and for enhancing your professionalism through participation in our Continuing Education Program.

International Investing: The Challenges and the Opportunities

Rodger F. Smith

INTRODUCTION

International investing by American pension funds is a relatively recent phenomenon. In many ways, the institutional part of the business was born in 1974 when Morgan Guaranty Trust launched the first commingled fund for pension funds to invest in international securities.

The birth was controversial in several ways. First, 1974 was the beginning of life with ERISA—a formalization of prudence. This new law created major turmoil among plan sponsors. Second, it came at the end of a two-year period of rapidly declining domestic equity prices, in 1973 and 1974. Third, Morgan Guaranty did not ask its clients for approval. Instead, clients that did not want international exposure were forced to say "no," which was in keeping with Morgan Guaranty's traditional sense of responsibility.

In hindsight, the timing of the move was almost perfect. The bottom of the market was reached very quickly, international performance in the early years was very strong, and the international investment management business as we know it today began to grow in earnest.

We have come a long way in just a decade. Much has been tried—and much more learned by plan sponsors and investment managers alike. The purpose of this seminar on International Equity Investing is to bring this learning together and to seek to channel future thought as the business moves from the rapid growth phase that has characterized it during the past several years into a more mature growth phase.

Before turning to a detailed examination of the business itself, it is useful to step back for a moment and look at the market forces that are driving the business—primarily America's largest pension funds. Pension funds are a trillion dollar business. They are also growing at an underlying rate of 12–15 percent per year. This rate of growth means that pension funds spawn a *new* business totalling nearly $150 billion each and every year. Truly, the business of managing pension funds is a very large, rapidly growing, and increasingly profitable business for investment management firms.

To put international investing by American pension funds into perspective, four different factors should be examined: first, the *number* of pension funds that invest abroad; second, the *dollars* they invest abroad today, and their intentions to change these investments in the future; third, the *reasons* pension funds invest internationally; and, fourth, the reasons pension funds do *not* invest internationally. This background will serve as a springboard for each of the subsequent speakers who will discuss more specific aspects of international investing.

INTERNATIONAL INVESTING BY AMERICAN PENSION FUNDS

The number of American pension funds investing internationally has increased significantly in recent years. Each year in the fall, Greenwich Research Associates conducts extensive research on the investment policies and practices used by large corporations in the management of their employee benefit funds. The Greenwich Research Associates universe includes the nation's 1,600 largest companies. These companies range from AT&T down to companies with plan assets as small as $10 million. In aggregate, their assets total more than $475 billion; they represent 80 percent of *all* corporate pension assets in America, and they account for the lion's share of the present dollars invested internationally.

More Plans Getting Involved

As shown in Table 1, the number of companies investing internationally more than doubled from 8 percent in 1979 to 17 percent in 1981. Growth slowed during the following two years with only a 1 percent increase each year to 18 percent in 1982 and to 19 percent this past year. This equates to approximately 250 large corporations that presently invest a portion of their employee benefit funds outside the United States.

Companies with larger plan assets more often invest internationally. Table 1 shows that almost two thirds of the companies with plan assets over

TABLE 1. How companies investing abroad have been changing

	1979	1980	1981	1982	1983
Plan assets					
Over $1 billion	26%	40%	59%	60%	63%
$251–1,000 million	21	25	35	40	31
$100–250 million	11	14	18	23	22
Under $100 million	3	6	8	9	6
Total companies	8	13	17	18	19

Source: Greenwich Research Associates.

$1 billion currently invest abroad. In contrast, approximately one-third of the companies with plan assets of $250 million to $1 billion invest abroad; one fifth of the companies with plan assets of $100 million to $250 million invest abroad; while only 6 percent of companies with plan assets under $100 million presently invest internationally. International investing is clearly a large-company phenomenon.

Dollar Commitment Is Growing Rapidly

Dollars invested abroad by corporate pension funds have also increased rapidly—and significant further growth is projected during the next three years. As shown in Table 2, pension assets invested internationally more than doubled from $4 billion in 1982 to almost $9 billion in 1983. This increase is ahead of last year's expectation of an increase to $8 billion in 1983. This is particularly interesting in light of the strong U.S. stock market and the strength of the dollar during that period.

Looking ahead, corporate pension funds expect to increase international investments more

TABLE 2. How projected dollars invested abroad have been changing

	1982 Actual	1983 Actual	1986 Projected
Plan assets			
Over $1 billion	$2,420*	$7,118	$17,346
$251–1,000 million	1,067	1,285	4,462
$100–250 million	313	288	775
Under $100 million	157	71	224
Total companies	$3,957	$8,761	$22,807

* Dollars in billions.
Source: Greenwich Research Associates.

than two and one-half times to a projected $23 billion by the end of 1986.

Assets invested internationally are concentrated among the very largest funds. In fact, 85 percent of present assets and 76 percent of projected 1986 assets are concentrated among companies with plan assets over $1 billion.

What is driving this expected $14 billion growth in assets invested internationally during the next three years? There are three different factors involved:

- Total pension assets (net contributions plus investment gains) are growing at an underlying rate of 12-15 percent per year. This "normal" growth in pension assets accounts for almost one-third of the projected growth of international assets from $9 billion in 1983 to $23 billion in 1986. With pension funds becoming increasingly well funded, a larger percentage of future growth will come from investment gains as opposed to net contributions.
- More companies are making initial commitments to international investing. In fact, 9 percent of the companies included in our 1983 research indicated they plan to *start* investing abroad by the end of 1984. This will bring the total number of companies investing internationally to approximately 375, assuming all these expectations are fulfilled. During the past four years, however, only 55 percent of the intentions to start investing abroad were actually fulfilled. Therefore, companies investing abroad for the first time account for slightly less than one-fifth of the total projected asset growth.
- Plan sponsors that presently invest abroad are increasing the *percent* of assets invested internationally. This increase in asset mix accounts for fully one-half of the projected $14 billion growth in international assets.

But Commitment Remains Low as Percentage of Total Assets

While international assets presently account for less than two percent of *total* employee benefit fund assets, the companies that invest abroad presently invest only slightly less than four percent of their assets internationally. As shown in Table 3, these companies plan to increase interna-

TABLE 3.	How percent of total assets invested internationally is changing		
	Percent invested	*1983 Actual*	*1986 Projected*
None		84.0%	71.0%
1		3.0	2.0
2		3.0	2.0
3		3.0	2.0
4		1.0	1.0
5		2.0	6.0
6–10		2.0	4.0
Over 10		0.0	0.0
No answer/uncertain		2.0	12.0
Mean*		3.8	5.6
Median		3.0	5.0

* Note: Mean and median exclude None.
Source: Greenwich Research Associates.

tional investments by 180 basis points to nearly six percent by the end of 1986. Interestingly, none of these funds now invest—or plan to invest—more than 10 percent of their total pension assets abroad. Because equity investments are 50 to 60 percent of total assets, international investments could total more than 10 percent of *equity* assets, but not more than 10 percent of *total* assets.

REASONS TO INVEST ABROAD: THEORY AND EVIDENCE

Corporate pension funds invest abroad for two primary, and complementary, reasons. To increase investment returns and to reduce total portfolio risk.

Initially, a majority of companies favored international investing as a way to reduce total portfolio risk by increasing diversification. As domestic equity markets improved, the pendulum began swinging the other way to the point where, in last year's research, reasons to invest abroad favored increasing returns over reducing risk by a 70 to 30 margin.

Return Experience

Empirical research shows that returns earned in international markets have exceeded returns earned domestically over long-time horizons. For the 10 year period 1973–1983, shown in Table 4, the compound annual rate of return for the Capital International EAFE index was 11.1 percent and outperformed the 10.6 percent return

TABLE 4.	Time weighted rates of return	
	Five years 1978–1983	*Ten years 1973–1983*
EAFE Index	10.1%	11.1%
S&P 500	17.3	10.6
CPI	8.4	8.2

of the S&P 500 by an average of 50 basis points annually over the entire period.

Relative to inflation, EAFE returns were also superior—outperforming the annual 8.2 percent increase in the Consumer Price Index by 290 basis points annually over the past decade.

During the past five years, however, the picture was different. For the period 1978–1983, the domestic market was strong with the S&P 500 return of 17.3 percent outperforming the 10.1 percent return of the EAFE Index by a whopping 720 basis points. During this same period, the EAFE Index again outperformed the 8.4 percent increase in the Consumer Price Index by an average of 170 basis points.

The long-term case for increased returns from international investing is strong. The past five years have not provided superior returns, but returns have exceeded the increase in consumer prices.

Risk Experience

Total portfolio risk has also been reduced by investing in international markets. As shown in Table 5, the standard deviation of the EAFE Index during the ten-year period, 1973–1983, was slightly higher than that of S&P 500—18.4 percent versus 18.2 percent. However, because returns from international markets are not highly correlated, total equity portfolio risk has been reduced by investing abroad. For example, by investing 10 percent of a domestic equity portfolio internationally, total equity portfolio risk was reduced to 17.8 percent—a decline in total equity

TABLE 5.	Standard deviation of returns
	Ten years 1973–1983
EAFE Index	18.4%
S&P 500	18.2
S&P/EAFE—90/10	17.8
S&P/EAFE—80/20	17.5

risk of a little more than two percent. By increasing the international component to 20 percent, total equity portfolio risk was further reduced to 17.5 percent, almost a four percent reduction in risk.

During the past ten years, therefore, domestic investors were rewarded for investing internationally both by increased returns and reduced risk.

REASONS NOT TO INVEST ABROAD

Corporate pension executives who do not invest abroad cite four reasons as most important in their decisions:

- Senior management reluctance;
- Lack of international experience internally;
- Foreign currency risk; and
- Political risks.

Interestingly, two concerns voiced by investment professionals about putting money abroad are not shared by plan sponsors. First, is the continued strength of the U.S. dollar. A number of investment organizations want to see the dollar weakened before committing assets abroad. This factor is not holding large corporations back.

A second concern to investment managers, but not to plan sponsors, is the perceived near-term attractiveness of the American stock market.

CONCLUSION

American pension funds have moved international investing from an emerging growth business into a new, but more mature growth business. More companies are investing abroad, more money is being invested abroad, and plan sponsors are increasing the percentage of assets invested internationally. All of these trends are currently positive, making the challenges facing plan sponsors and investment managers increasingly important—and exciting. With this as background, let's proceed now to look at the specific challenges of managing international portfolios.

International Diversification: Theory, Practice and Experience (I)

Gary L. Bergstrom

I'm not sure that my presentation is really "theory," because what I hope to do—while I'll bring theory into it from time to time—is relate more to the practical problems of investment managers. Specifically, I will focus on that important empirical evidence that international managers can utilize to develop and implement better equity management strategies.

My view is that confessions are good for the soul, even in the investment management business. So, before I present some thoughts on the current status and possible future directions of international equity investment, I would like to tell you a few of my prejudices on the subject, and a little about where they may have come from. I have been associated with international investing through a number of different organizations since the early 1970s, both as an international portfolio manager and as a consultant. I have also been involved in hiring, and occasionally firing, international investment managers. Over the years I have developed a number of reasonably strong opinions on the subject. So be forewarned.

In terms of a focus for my remarks, our firm is now in the process of implementing a new active international equity management strategy. This has given us an opportunity to go back to the drawing board, taking into account both experience and recent theoretical developments. It has also allowed us to think in a reasonably unfettered fashion about how a manager might go about designing and implementing a better active international strategy. In particular, it has given us some ideas on approaches to international equity management that may have value over the long term.

ENVIRONMENTAL ISSUES IN INVESTING ABROAD

First of all, let's talk a little bit about the investment environment abroad as we see it, in terms of state-of-the-art investment practice. Consider the following *opinions* on the current state of international equity management.

- Most investors abroad are still 5 to 20 years behind the most sophisticated U.S. managers.
- Large banks still dominate some markets.
- Top down and stock picking are the most prevalent investment strategies.
- Most managers favor higher growth markets and larger capitalization issues.
- There are few true contrarians or value oriented players.
- Transaction costs are still generally high by U.S. standards.
- Few high quality computer-readable data bases exist as yet.
- There has been limited use to date of analytical techniques in non-U.S. markets.

These are some of the environmental issues that we think investment managers should think about when they start to develop what is hoped will be better, more effective equity management strategies.

THE PERFORMANCE RECORD

Absolute and Relative Return Data

There are a number of sources of recent historical evidence about active international equity managers and what sort of results they've had. Ours is Wood, McKenzie & Company in London. In looking at their universe of active equity managers over the past four years, a number of points are worth noting. First of all, their universe, which is some 150 dollar-denominated equity funds, had a higher standard deviation of return than the Capital International Index over the same period of time. In fact, a little over 1.1 times the standard deviation. Second, as we'll see more clearly in Figure 1, even if one had invested equally in the Wood, MacKenzie universe of 150 managed portfolios, one would, over this period have been quite undiversified, relative to the Capital International Europe, Australia, and Far

FIGURE 1
Quarterly performance differential between CIEAFE Index and non-U.S. median

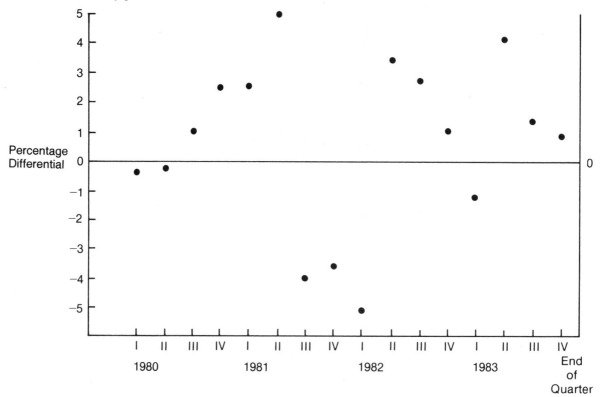

East Index (CIEAFE). Now, that means one of two things: Either the CIEAFE Index isn't a very good proxy for non-U.S. markets—and I think that's part of the answer—or active international equity managers as a group have been weighting their portfolios and doing things quite differently from that Index.

Finally, the good news—and we always need some positives. Over the four years ending December 31, 1983, the Wood, MacKenzie aggregate outperformed the CIEAFE Index by almost four percent per annum. However, it also underperformed the S&P 500 by 1.9 percent per annum over the same period.

One small numerical note: By our statistics, in the last two or three months the international aggregate has outperformed the S&P 500 to the extent that the 1.9 percent per annum lag may very well be close to zero by this point, if you were to look at the 17-quarter period ending March 31, 1984.

Figure 1 simply illustrates that, in general, the Wood, MacKenzie universe of managers has been relatively undiversified versus the CIEAFE Index. You see that there have been quite a number of quarters over the last four years where

that aggregate has been four percent or more, either above or below the Index. Again, this suggests that there may well be some problems with that index as a representative measure for non-U.S. equity portfolios.

"PRODUCT DESIGN" CONSIDERATIONS FOR NON–U.S. INVESTING

I would like now to turn to some specifics of what we like to call product design considerations. In particular, for the active international equity manager who is interested in maximizing his chances of investment success over the long term, we think there are a number of points that merit consideration—these are points from theory, if you will, which relate to structuring more productive international equity management strategies.

Diversification: The International Correlation Structure

The first of these theoretical considerations goes back to one of the earliest arguments for international equity diversification—namely, the basic covariance argument. The question is always raised, "Well, aren't non-U.S. markets moving more in sync with the U.S. now? Doesn't this erode a lot of the rationale for diversification into non-U.S. markets?" We have some evidence on that subject that we should examine closely.

Table I provides three sets of historical correlation numbers between the U.S. market and other major world markets. All of these numbers were calculated from data in the pre-1975 period. They were published in *The Journal of Portfolio Management* in 1975, so we don't have any "look ahead" bias in terms of the statistical calculations. I would, in particular, call your attention to the correlation coefficients in the right-most column that Lessard prepared. Again, they were published in 1975, based on Capital International Market indexes data from 1959 through the latter part of 1973. As you can see, a number of markets like Canada and the Netherlands had, over these periods of time, fairly high correlations with the U.S. market. Markets like Spain and the South African gold mines had generally low correlations.

Now, the key question is whether the international correlation structure situation has changed dramatically with more recent data. Using statistics for the two-year period ending December 31, 1983 and sorting the data by correlation versus the Standard & Poor's 500, we have

TABLE 2. Acadian Financial Research (Period ending December 31, 1983)

Index for:	Standard deviat.*	Beta versus S&P 500	Corr. versus S&P 500†
USA	14.8	1.00	0.99
World	12.7	0.80	0.92
Canada	24.3	1.27	0.76
Netherlands	20.0	0.74	0.54
Singapore	20.0	0.73	0.53
Eur., Australia, Far East	14.0	0.47	0.49
Belgium	17.3	0.53	0.45
United Kingdom	14.5	0.42	0.42
Switzerland	15.4	0.44	0.41
Norway	27.4	0.77	0.41
Denmark	19.9	0.56	0.41
Japan	22.1	0.58	0.38
Austria	15.0	0.33	0.32
Australia	26.5	0.56	0.31
France	18.2	0.35	0.28
Germany	19.6	0.29	0.22
Sweden	26.1	0.35	0.19
Italy	20.6	0.25	0.18
Spain	17.8	0.15	0.13
Mexico	83.9	−0.71	−0.12
Hong Kong	43.4	−0.54	−0.19

* Annualized Basis.
† Volatility and correlation estimates based upon 24 months of data ending 12/83.

here again the Capital International Market index in Table 2. How do these numbers compare with the three earlier sets that we looked at? First, Canada once again has the highest correlation with the U.S. market. Spain is again down at the low end in terms of correlation, while the Netherlands is again relatively high. Although there is certainly a far from precise matching with the earlier numbers, generally there haven't been any particularly dramatic shifts in terms of the international covariance structure, given the inherent uncertainty in statistical estimation techniques.

In Table 3, some correlation coefficients between developing markets and the U.S. market over the 1976 to 1980 time frame are shown. The basic conclusion is that the typical correlation coefficients between developing markets and the U.S. market are lower than those between the U.S. and the major European and Far East markets. Looking at the names of those developing markets provides ample evidence for predicting that we won't see any major U.S. institutional investors doing much in this sector over at least the next five years.

TABLE 1. Correlations versus U.S. market

Market	Grubel*	Solnik†	Lessard‡
Australia	.06	—	.23
Austria	—	—	.12
Belgium	.11	.47	.46
Canada	.70	—	.80
Denmark	—	—	.04
France	.19	.06	.25
Germany	.30	.22	.38
Italy	.15	.07	.21
Japan	.11	.19	.13
Netherlands	.21	.51	.61
Norway	—	—	.17
S. African Gold Mines	.16	—	—
Spain	—	—	.04
Sweden	—	.29	.33
Switzerland	—	.44	.49
United Kingdom	.24	.20	.29

* Grubel Data: 1959–1966; Published 1968.
† Solnik Data: 3/66–4/71; Published 1973.
‡ Lessard Data: 1/59–10/73; Published 1975.
Source: The Journal of Portfolio Management.

TABLE 3. Correlation coefficients monthly U.S. $ total returns (1976–1980) U.S. market versus—

Spain	0.11
Hong Kong	0.27
Singapore	0.42
Argentina	−0.02
Brazil	−0.03
Chile	−0.18
Greece	−0.01
Jordan	0.34
Korea	0.23
Mexico	0.22
Thailand	−0.36
Zimbabwe	0.00

Source: Errunza, *Emerging Markets: A New Opportunity for Improving Global Portfolio Performance,* Financial Analysts Journal, 1983.

As an aside, there are now more sophisticated and accurate analytical techniques for predicting the future correlation structure between markets. We have a model which uses weekly Capital International data and does some rather fancier statistical operations that seems to predict the short-term correlation structure between world markets quite a bit better than more traditional measures that simply use historical monthly data.

"Small-Stock" Considerations

Having looked at the correlation argument, the next matter to consider in designing international equity management strategies is the so-called "small-stock" effect. Most professionals are probably familiar with that notion in the United States. Internationally, there is not a great deal of direct empirical evidence on this subject as yet—certainly not up to U.S. standards. But it's still a very important consideration for several reasons.

Just briefly recapping the U.S. empirical evidence, a careful study done a couple of years ago found that between 1926 and 1980 all New York Stock Exchange issues with a market value of less than $50 million returned 2.8 percent per annum more than larger capitalization issues. Likewise, during the 56-year period from 1926 through 1981, it was found that the annualized total rate of return for the S&P 500 was about 9.1 percent, but for smaller companies on the New York Stock Exchange over this same period, there was a total rate of return of 12.1 percent.

With the exception of Japan, there isn't any direct evidence that would suggest that the same thing is happening in non-U.S. markets. The data really only goes back to the late 1960s in any reasonably cohesive form. Nonetheless, it would not be unreasonable, in my judgment, to find an analogous size effect in at least a number of non-U.S. equity markets. Moreover, when considering smaller companies outside the United States, they are much more likely to offer the U.S. investor substantial diversification possibilities simply because their business results are usually less influenced by worldwide economic factors than those of very large corporations.

Large portfolio managers of international equities are probably not in a very good position to take advantage of the small-stock effect, even if it is as significant. But for smaller managers developing their strategies, it is a consideration, particularly when we look at the composition of most actively managed international portfolios and note that they are typically quite heavily invested in major companies.

Developing-Country Markets

Several other points that merit consideration would include the idea that the so-called developing-country markets, at least conceptually, seem to offer another intriguing way of possibly increasing return per unit of risk in an international equity portfolio. Errunza[1] studied many of these markets over the period from 1976 through 1980. One of his empirical findings was that a broadly diversified strategy of investing equally in 15 industrialized markets abroad, plus 12 developing-country markets, returned about 11 percent per annum above the Standard & Poor's 500, with less portfolio volatility. That's one of those nice theoretical constructs. It doesn't take into account things such as transactions costs and a lot of the other practical problems, but it is suggestive of the fact that, at least in the long-term, perhaps more international equity managers should be broadening their horizons to newer, developing markets.

Even so, as stated earlier, there will probably be virtually no activity on the part of major U.S. institutions in those sectors, with possibly the occasional exception of a small foray into Mexico or, of course, Hong Kong and Singapore. Again, when one thinks about developing-country mar-

---

[1] Errunza, "Emerging Markets: A New Opportunity for Improving Global Portfolio Performance." *Financial Analysts Journal,* 1983.

kets, it's obviously not the kind of strategy that one can consider seriously for very large amounts of assets. But, there may very well be some potentials for adding value to moderate sized portfolios.

The Importance of a Systematic Valuation Process

Another very important issue in international equity management strategies is the use of some sort of systematic, analytical valuation process. Even if it's very crude and oversimplified, it can be of significant value. We all know there are major problems with the availability of data, with inflation-induced distortions, and with accounting differentials across countries. Nonetheless, since we're in a relative competition for adding investment value, and most other investors face the same problems, one should endeavor to develop and implement some sensible valuation processes, even though they may be much less sophisticated than ones used in the United States.

A Valuation Model Example

To give you an example of what I'm talking about, I would like to describe a particular quantitative valuation process we developed a few years ago. It is a process that has been used since 1981 to manage institutional money, so we do have some actual operational history as well as a number of years of simulation history. This description will illustrate what I mean by systematic, analytical valuation processes in what we all acknowledge is a difficult area.

Its basic structure is that of a dividend-discount model, done on a very aggregated basis. It attempts to evaluate the overall attractiveness of each of the major national equity markets in the Capital International universe. Within each country, the portfolio is designed to track reasonably close the local Capital International Index. There are no judgments made of individual security valuation levels. Again, the only active management judgments are made at the macro level when assessing a particular national market's attractiveness.

The dividend-discount model itself is a classic three-stage model, with explicit forecasts over the next year, which is about as far ahead as we thought we could reasonably forecast such

variables as dividends and earnings. There is a transition period of varying length, depending upon the national economy and our view of its degree of maturity. Finally, there's a terminal period where we assume, rather heroically, that certain static conditions will continue.

The important inputs used to derive a stream of estimated future dividends for each market include, first and foremost, our forecast of real GNP growth by country. By making some simplifying assumptions and concentrating on real GNP growth, we avoid having to make forecasts of exchange rate shifts; we bring everything back into real terms and assume that currency markets in the long term are reasonably efficient. We also make estimates of the current inflation-adjusted book value and earnings for each national Capital International Market Index when possible.

Obviously, making these kinds of adjustments is not a simple process. But, when one goes back into the archives and does some homework, there's more data available on at least a half-dozen major economies around the world than many managers suspect. It is, I would warn you, a rather labor-intensive activity—but you do get some intriguing insights.

Another input is estimates of future earnings for each national market index. Again, we make some adjustments to the stated Capital International earnings numbers for things like inventories, depreciation, and debt. That is, again, done only on a country-by-country basis. Finally, one also needs some terminal period assumptions about return on equity and growth rate for this particular model.

Applying Judgment and Some Results

In practice, the outputs of the model are applied to the portfolio management process along with considerable subjective judgments by investment professionals. While no means an automated process, it does provide useful insights and an overall valuation discipline that I think is extremely helpful. To complete the operation we use some explicit portfolio optimization models in order to choose final portfolio weights, taking into consideration judgmental factors as well as the numerical estimates derived from the dividend-discount model.

Table 4 shows some recent examples of the sort of country portfolio weightings that ensue from the methodology just described. As I think

TABLE 4. Recent portfolio country weightings		
Country	CIEAFE weighting	Portfolio weighting
Australia	5.0%	4.2%
France	3.6	6.3
Germany	9.0	18.0
Hong Kong	1.9	3.0
Japan	48.1	32.3
Netherlands	3.9	8.8
Singapore	3.0	0
Switzerland	4.7	3.9
United Kingdom	20.8	23.5

the numbers suggest to all of us, this model basically tends to drive us to be contrarians in terms of the markets that we favor. There was a long period when Hong Kong kept showing up very unfavorably on this model. But last fall a switch occurred and it showed up at an attractive-enough level to justify an overweighted position. Likewise, Japan has been rather consistently out of favor with this particular market valuation approach in recent years. The basic thrust of what we're trying to do here is make relatively modest overweights and underweights on national market indexes while carefully controlling risk so that the risk of the aggregate portfolio is very close to that of the CIEAFE index itself.

Table 4 provides some simulated and actual results for this model. The year 1975 probably deserves brief mention. As of the end of 1974, the model favored the U.K. market to the maximum extent permitted by the portfolio optimizer. This was based upon its appraisal of the attractiveness of that market. In 1975 that market was up well over 100 percent. That accounts in part for the strategy's very substantial outperformance in that year. Also, for those of you who follow dividend-discount type models in the U.S. market, it might be interesting to note that in 1980 they didn't work very well for U.S. issues, either.

A LOOK AT THE FUTURE

I have a few additional remarks that I will lump under the label "Future Trends in International Equity Investing." First of all, I predict that over the next 5 to 10 years we are going to see increasing development and use for non-U.S. markets of analytical models and techniques of the types that are now reasonably commonplace in the United States. Obviously, for that to happen, one needs extensive, accurate, computer-readable data bases, which still, by and large, are not available in most foreign markets. There is, however, some excellent progress in Japan on that front and in the United Kingdom. This data will provide a very necessary infrastructure element to facilitate development of future tools.

Some specific examples of the kind of models and techniques we are going to see include models for estimating the sensitivity of company and portfolio earnings growth rates to key macroeconomic factors such as real GNP growth, models such as the one referred to above in a very simplified form. Also, there will be models to help one assess the sensitivity of earnings growth to such factors as inflation, wage rates, energy costs, and so forth. These will follow up some of the work that Tony Estep, Stephen Ross and others have done here in the United States.

I think various types of formal valuation models, including dividend-discount models and others, for calculating expected returns and durations for individual stocks under various assumptions will become more common. I know of a few pioneers who are doing work in that area now. We, for example, are working on adapting the dividend-discount type framework to individual companies abroad. This is a very ambitious undertaking, both as to the data collection and the analytical modeling. I also think that there will be increasing use of explicit portfolio optimization models for constructing efficient portfolios in risk-return terms—once again, when the data becomes available.

In terms of some final conclusions, looking at the international investment scene from a detached perspective, I find it fascinating that certain U.S. equity managers with extremely successful long-term performance records have been routinely investing major portions of their total portfolios in non-U.S equities since at least the 1960s. Looking to the future, perhaps in the next ten years or so many of us ordinary mortals will be doing the same thing. In fact, I will be so bold as to predict that in the not-too-distant future, almost all sophisticated U.S. equity managers will routinely consider investments in non-U.S. stocks as part of their ordinary investment management process. It won't be at all unheard of to see 50 percent or more of a "domestic" equity portfolio invested in non-U.S. stocks, under certain kinds of market conditions.

In such an environment, if you believe that brave forecast, I think discussion of non-U.S. investment opportunities will be almost a standard part of every major domestic investment meeting. The sort of specialized seminar we have here, devoted primarily to international investing, will eventually go out of fashion. Well-trained managers will grow up investing abroad as naturally as investing at home.

International Diversification: Theory, Practice, and Experience (II)

William P. Marshall

As we think back on the last four or five years, we can see that it's been a very exciting experience. As Gary Bergstrom mentioned, confessions can be good for the soul. I think today we all have an opportunity to get a bit of a soul cleansing done as we go back and reflect on it all.

I'm happy to share with you our experience in the international investment sphere. After some remarks that will explain GTE's rationale for investing abroad—for starting it—I'll talk a bit about implementation, historical results, some future anticipations, and then provide a summary and conclusions.

ONE COMPANY'S ROUTE TO INVESTMENT ABROAD

Our rationale for investing abroad is simply that we saw a higher ROI potential. We saw this more than five years ago, feeling that there would be stronger prosperity in some other countries, basically coming from higher productivity and unit growth, and better monetary control for limited inflation.

Actually, if we had to do this again, I think

we might even go a little further and see if we couldn't concoct some sort of prosperity measures. For instance, if you think of prosperity as being good productivity and no inflation, then subtracting inflation away from productivity may give you some measure of prosperity. Perhaps we may yet do this, to get a better handle on international investment characteristics.

We also saw opportunities for increased diversification. The rest of the world is as big as the U.S. equity market, and there is the power of covariance. That is, very simply, the counteraction of local market movements as well as fluctuations in the different currencies.

Putting it all together into the capital market framework of Figure 1 shows what we've perceived. On the vertical scale is the annualized *real* rate of return. We like to think in terms of real rate of return because inflation is really our major bogey. We have an advance funding operation for future pension liabilities, which behaves as an extension of the payroll. We know we must stay well ahead of inflation if we are to satisfy the requirements of the plan.

So, we think in terms of real rate of return. We felt that the S&P 500, after looking at many decades of data, was good for about a 5 percent real rate of return, with maybe a 20 percent standard deviation. We felt that international equities would be good for perhaps a little bit more return, based on the stronger prosperity that we perceived in other countries, and would also provide a bit of a reduced risk level because of the workings of covariance within that very broad universe.

With this in mind, about six years ago we were working on a study. We looked at ERISA, got some legal opinions, and concluded that ERISA's diversification language embraced the international sphere. With that sort of a tailwind, we went on to look at other factors. We felt that because the international arena was as big as the United States, there had to be ample liquidity. A study of the literature even five or six years ago provided enough data to make this

FIGURE 1

Anticipated performance characteristics

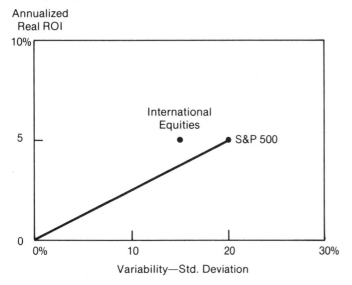

conclusion firm. We also decided that currency fluctuations tend to cancel out. We had to look at many historical series and so-called "spaghetti graphs" to reach this conclusion. In the end, we felt that currency fluctuations would not be a problem to worry about.

Please note that investing in multinational firms is not really what we're looking for. That doesn't provide sufficient diversification. When investing in multinationals, you do get some of the effect on fundamentals, in terms of the currency effects on earnings and so forth, but for the most part they are traded on the New York Stock Exchange and it is very hard to get away from that influence. That's why we felt we had to do more.

The theory is that political risks can't be correctly anticipated by markets, so political risk is always present. Markets are efficient enough and as soon as they perceive political difficulties they will sell off accordingly, but the occurrence of the risks cannot really be accurately foreseen. However, political risks can be diversified away by exposure across a number of countries. When one country is down, another one is up. Again, covariance comes into play, just as it does on currency.

Finally, we reached the conclusion that investment costs would be reasonable. We recognized that there would be higher transaction costs: brokerage commissions, custodian costs, investment management fees, and so on. They would be higher in other lands, but not so high that we couldn't get a positive net advantage over the market after all costs.

Implementing the Program

After this analysis, we wound up with a recommendation that a combination of active and passive investment approaches to international investment would be an appropriate step for GTE to take. So saying, we began the program in early 1979 with a passive approach, using index funds at State Street Bank & Trust Co. We also made some trips to London and were impressed with the investment expertise we found in the United Kingdom. Then, feeling that it would also be desirable to have some active managers, we started with three before subsequently adding more.

We had two modes of operation for the managers to choose from: world portfolios and EAFE portfolios. Most managers chose the world op-

eration, because they perceived that they were global in scope. Some managers, however, said that they preferred EAFE, so we've set up these two universes accordingly. At present, world exposure is about three quarters of the entire program.

Finally, we added a couple of fixed-income managers in 1983. I recognize that this is an equity seminar, but our overall program does have a bit of fixed income content. We also have an insurance company in Bermuda that has a multi-currency investment program which was initiated in 1982. All together, that is the scope of our international operations.

In hiring managers we look at several major factors that we call the "Four P's."

Professionalism	The firm
	Skills
	Dedication
Processes for decision-making	Philosophy & approach
	Strategic development
	Portfolio procedures
Portfolio strategy	Regional allocation
	Asset mix
	Issues
Performance	Characteristics
	Allocation
	Selection

The first factor is professionalism. We want to understand all we can about the firm: how viable it is and what kind of environment it has. We want to understand the skills of its people and what they're really best at. We want to understand what makes them run. Dedication is very important. We are very interested in such things as compensation and overall team spirit.

We very definitely want to understand what they do and how they do it, including their decision-making processes. We like to know the philosophy and approach—what they feel is the best way to get the performance they anticipate. We like to know how they develop strategy and what techniques they have that evidence discriminatory power within the different markets that they go into. And, of course, we like to assure ourselves that the portfolio procedures are sound and that we will be on the receiving end of a quality product from a firm whose outcomes across its customer base are not widely dispersed.

After we get into a program with a manager, we want to understand as much as we can about their portfolio strategy. We like to know how the regional allocation is set up—what it is and why it came into being—and we want to know what the asset mix is within countries. In some countries, nonequity assets play a fairly significant role.

Finally, when it comes to performance, we want to understand as much as we can about its aggregate characteristics, in terms of R-squares, residual return, and residual standard deviation, and such other types of statistics. We are working very hard at developing an attribution system that will let us understand the components of performance in terms of the impact coming from allocation decisions and the impact coming from selection decisions.

Parenthetically, although we've only been at it for a couple of years and this may be a bit of a surprising conclusion, it appears that allocation is more or less a neutral element, and that the major successes come from selecting well within major markets. If you go to Japan, which is a major market, obviously you want to select well, because that's going to have a major impact on the bottom line. The same holds true within the United States and within the United Kingdom. It's a bit less important when it comes to some of the smaller markets, but yet, in toto, you obviously want to select well.

Maybe some of you have read the book, *In Search of Excellence,* which portrayed a number of U.S. corporations and tried to capture some of the things they were doing well. The book made eight points, one of which was to be close to the customer. I think that in this particular business we could add a ninth point: be close to your manager. You really need to know the qualitative and quantitative aspects of what's going on. That's why we run a farm team—to get that type of education.

Where the Program Stands

Let's look at a summary of our program as it stood at the end of last year. As shown in Table 1, the pension portion had $309 million in U.S. dollars in equity and $32 million in fixed income, for a total of $341 million internationally. You can see on the right the nondollar content versus the index. For the total we are 65 percent nondollar, versus 60 percent for the index, so we are 5 percent nondollar tilted. This tilt comes from the pension managers' strategies, on which we have

TABLE 1. Summary of international investment programs as of December 31, 1983

	$ Millions U.S.	Non-dollar Content	Non-dollar Index	Non-dollar Diff.
Pension (out of $5 billion)				
Equity	$309	63%	56%	7%
Fixed income	32	75	100	−25
Total Pension	341	65	60	5
Insurance	94	26	21	5
Composite	$435	56%	51%	5%

no particular influence. In the insurance company, which has a slightly different thrust—it's more debt-oriented—there is a 26 percent nondollar content, versus 21 percent for its index. Again, that's a five percent nondollar tilt. The composite program of $435 million is 56 percent nondollar, versus 51 percent for the index. We think that's a very appropriate stance, given what we envision in the future.

An Unexpected Development

Having seen how we've implemented this program and where it stands now, let's do a little soul-searching and look at an environmental factor that happened along the way. Figure 2 shows performance characteristics for the past four and three-quarters years: annualized real rate of return on the vertical scale and variability, in terms of standard deviation, on the horizontal scale. Going from the origin up to the S&P, which provided about a 10 percent real rate of return with about an 18 percent standard deviation—that's a very nice outcome—we see that EAFE, in local-return terms, had just a little bit lower rate of return, with a considerably smaller standard deviation. As plotted, it is above the capital market line (from the origin through the S&P return) and, hence, has an implied residual return. That's as we would have expected.

What we didn't expect was that EAFE, in *dollar* terms, would behave in a disappointing fashion by providing only a small real return at a variability near 20 percent. As we go back and rack our brains over it, looking again at everything available to look at five years ago, would we have done it? I think we have to come up with "Yes" as a conclusion. What did we not foresee? We did not foresee Paul Volcker in the

Fed squeezing and relaxing alternately. We did not see President Reagan coming in and creating the extended Reaganomics that has transpired. I think both of these factors probably have contributed in a major way to the strengthening of the dollar and, hence, to the weakening of the EAFE currency cocktail.

PERFORMANCE MONITORING AND MEASUREMENT EVALUATION CRITERIA

Looking more specifically at our results (see Table 2), five years ago we had $36 million internationally, having just gotten the program started. In the subsequent four and three-quarters years, we've added $235 million of GTE money and experienced a total return of $164 million, bringing us to the ending market value of $435 million. Performance has been quite satisfactory. Return on investment, total return, appreciation, and income, is at 14.1 percent per year; our benchmark performance index for the overall international program was 12.7 percent per year. From that we derive a variance-from-benchmark (VFB) of plus 1.4 percent per year. So, we have reason to be pleased about the way security selection has been progressing in this program.

TABLE 2. Overall international composite summary of investment results through December 31, 1983

Reconciliation ($ millions U.S.)	
Beginning market value—3/31/79	$ 36
Net additions	235
Total return	164
Ending market value—12/31/83	$435
Performance (annualized)	
Return on investment—percent ROI	14.1%
Benchmark—performance index, Overall international	12.7
Variance from benchmark—VFB	1.4%

We anchor all of our GTE investment programs to performance indexes. The composite used for the international program is a cocktail of indexes that we track ourselves against, internationally. Performance-wise, over the long period of time, while there has been a bit of variabil-

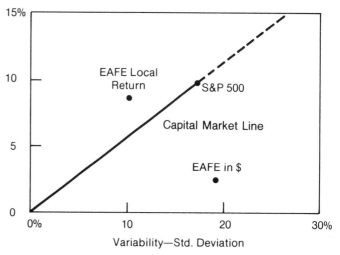

FIGURE 2
Performance characteristics (March 31, 1979 to Dec. 31, 1983)

ity in results, basically the composite program is ahead of the performance index and both are ahead of inflation, as shown in Figure 3. We have enjoyed a particularly fine real rate of return. I certainly hope that we can continue it, although we have to recognize that there will be variability along the way.

Assessing Results to Date

Looking at performance now in terms of a "variance-from-benchmark" index, where we simply divide the index into the unit value series to get a relative strength readout, you can see in Figure 4 the variability mentioned earlier. It was particularly evident in 1981, when things seemed to be falling out of bed a bit. It is necessary to have a longer-term perspective on inflation to take a look at graphics such as this.

Looking further back at some of the historical characteristics of this index, we see in Figure 5 the real rate of return (on the vertical scale) for different components of the index as well as the return on the S&P, with a capital market line drawn in. For the past 14 years, the S&P has given a 2 percent real rate of return, thanks to 1973 and 1974. Other than that it was pretty much tracking our original five percent per year expectation. The EAFE index was a little bit more volatile, but it did provide the desired higher rate of return. There is an implied positive residual:

FIGURE 3
Overall international composite and performance index (March 31, 1979 to December 31, 1983)

Unit Values

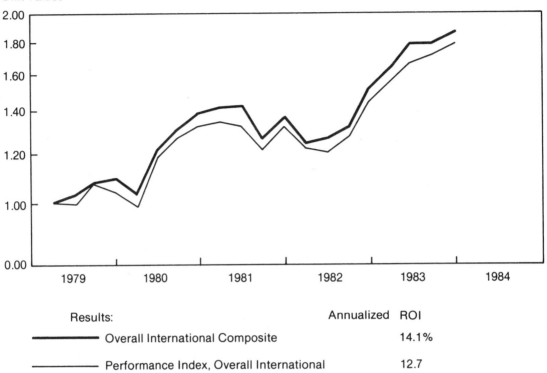

Results:	Annualized ROI
——— Overall International Composite	14.1%
——— Performance Index, Overall International	12.7

FIGURE 4
Overall international composite versus performance index (March 31, 1979 to December 31, 1983)

Variance from Benchmark Index

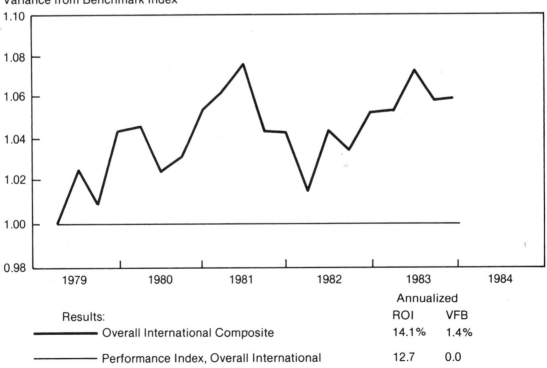

Results:	Annualized ROI	VFB
——— Overall International Composite	14.1%	1.4%
——— Performance Index, Overall International	12.7	0.0

FIGURE 5
Historical performance characteristics (14 years ended
December 31, 1983)

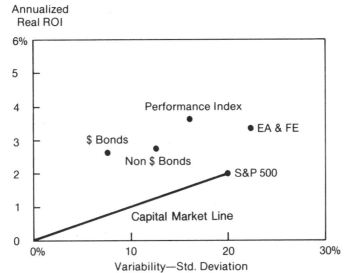

FIGURE 6
Composite investment program notional index versus inflation (December 31, 1969 to December 31, 1983)

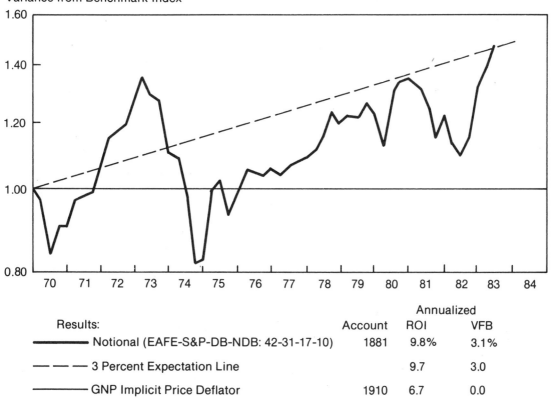

Results:	Account	Annualized ROI	VFB
———— Notional (EAFE-S&P-DB-NDB: 42-31-17-10)	1881	9.8%	3.1%
— — — 3 Percent Expectation Line		9.7	3.0
———— GNP Implicit Price Deflator	1910	6.7	0.0

Jensen's alpha, if you will. The nonequity areas, the dollar bonds and the nondollar bonds, also produced attractive returns during that time, variability considered.

Put them all together and you see that the performance index actually had a slightly higher return than the components which make it up. That comes from the benefits of covariance and continuous rebalancing. When we run the 14-year model this way, we rebalance every quarter without transaction costs. The rebalancing is one of the latent benefits inherent in international investing. Another way to look at variance-from-benchmark is to let inflation be the benchmark, as shown in Figure 6. This shows the great amount of variability in this series, particularly in 1973 and 1974. Taking a longer-term perspective, however, this index roughly tracks the three percent expectation. We often overlay "expectation lines" on our graphs to give us an additional frame of reference.

FUTURE EXPECTATIONS

Well, so much for looking back. Looking forward, what do we see? The currency factor is obviously a somewhat larger element than we originally

thought five years ago. We think of this factor not in terms of the strength of the dollar, but in terms of the strength of the underlying currency cocktail that is part of the EAFE return. There are several factors that we see possibly hardening and softening the EAFE currency cocktail. There's a growing trade deficit which is presumably going to affect dollars going abroad to purchase other currencies. That ought to have hardening influence at some point. There is a large federal deficit at a record high of maybe five percent or six percent of GNP. We've never had anything like that before; but other countries, such as Japan, Germany, and Canada, have had similarly-proportioned public sector deficits and seem to have adapted all right. This is a new ball game for the United States and the question is, does it imply increased monetarization on the part of the Fed? If it does, that probably will increase inflationary pressures, which will work through purchasing power parity to the disadvantage of the dollar and to the advantage of the other countries.

There are, however, some softening influences. We have very high real interest rates in the United States. That, of course, is bringing back a return flow of capital to counteract the

FIGURE 7
EA&FE major currency cocktail (December 31, 1973 to December 31, 1989)

Unit Values

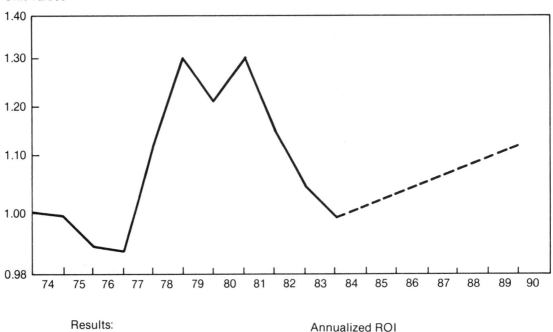

Results:	Annualized ROI
——— EA&FE Major Currency Cocktail	0.7%

trade deficit. There is also a high level of confidence in the political stability of the United States. I think Reagan's popularity has been fairly steady over the past four years. Then you have a strong Fed stance on inflation. Chairman Volcker went to the Fed four or five years ago and throughout this period obviously has had an extreme interest in inflation.

Putting currency into graphic form to see where things might go, Figure 7 shows an appropriate EAFE currency cocktail that we've derived from our computer system. By picking currency prices out of the newspaper and using EAFE weights, we've been able to go back about ten years and take the currency element out of the EAFE performance series. When we do, it looks like this, a little like the trade-weighted dollar and other series that you may have seen.

In the period of 1974 to 1976, the currency cocktail was weakening a bit, but then the so-called Carter dollar came in and it got very strong. Then, toward the end of 1981, it fell out of bed. Of course, the currency cocktail was strongest just when we began our program. That might make one feel a bit silly, except that after going back and looking at everything we could have looked at when we started this, we still feel it was the right thing to do. Even though this came along, it's just an aspect of political/currency risk that—over time—should melt away.

In the future, as the dashed line on Figure 7 shows, we think maybe we might get as much as two percent annual growth out of this currency cocktail, which is an add-on to the local return from the EAFE countries. That's a very cautious forecast; it's sort of a consensus forecast that comes from our own internal international economics department, from talking with managers, and so forth. I worry about this a little bit. If there's too much consensus in there, the consensus has a way of being painted silly more often than not.

In conclusion, as we look at it all, we find that international investing offers an attractive performance potential. We definitely expect a higher rate of return with lower variability. The opportunity for enriching a plan's overall investment talent is also substantial. We're very impressed with the investment professionalism that we find in the United Kingdom, and as we become more knowledgeable about the rest of the world, I am confident that we will find equally high levels of professionalism elsewhere.

The strength of the dollar has been our biggest surprise, but we think it could weaken in the next few years. Putting it all together, we think it's appropriate to increase our pension fund's nondollar commitment beyond the present four percent. In the context of Rodger Smith's research we seek to be in the ballpark and, like others, are thinking about boosting our future exposure a bit.

Bergstrom/Marshall Q & A Session

MODERATOR: I thought Gary Bergstrom did a good job building the case that managers can beat the EAFE index by investing in small stocks and in developing countries. But, looking at less adventuresome approaches, what I would really like to know is whether the theoretical case for international investing is still sound and whether the EAFE index can beat the S&P. Will this possibility be reduced as more and more funds invest internationally, as opposed to just domestically?

GARY BERGSTROM: In terms of the risk reduction issue, first of all, I think that the correlation coefficients we were looking at a little while ago, as well as some of Bill Marshall's evidence, suggest that you can still reduce risk by investing internationally, if you do it in a careful, thoughtful, and systematic fashion. On the return side, I think if we've learned anything over the last 10 years in this area—and some of Bill's data again shows this—it is that there is a lot of variability in the performance of the U.S. market versus the EAFE index. Just as there is a lot of variability in the relative returns across markets—which is what you would expect when you look at those correlation coefficients.

On a prospective basis I can tell you that, where we have a great deal of freedom in how we manage and where we invest abroad, the data we're looking at have been suggesting for some time that a number of foreign markets are in fact better values than the U.S. market. While a lot of that has been rectified over the last three months, with foreign markets up a number of percentage points while the U.S. market is down rather sharply, there probably still is more value yet in the non-U.S. indexes versus the U.S. market.

QUESTION: So it looks like the returns will in fact be higher?

GARY BERGSTROM: That's a good guess.

QUESTION: You talked about stock selection and you talked about country selection. But you didn't talk about currency management. Is it possible to add value through currency management, and if so, how?

GARY BERGSTROM: There was a major reason why I didn't go too far into the currency side. That is, while I wish I could say we've developed some great ways to forecast currencies, I really can't make any such claims. There may be some people who are quite good at all that, but we don't claim to be. If one looks at the usual purchasing power parity kinds of analyses that everybody else looks at, one sees the dollar looking very robust. But trying to forecast the relative movements of different currencies against one another and the dollar is another matter.

Parenthetically, on the subject of analyzing currencies, Professor Lessard at MIT has done some very interesting work, pointing out a theoretical structure for looking at the effects of currency changes on equities. The basic point he makes is that if you're going to try to decompose or back currency returns out from equity market returns, you should not look at changes in exchange rates more or less concurrently with changes in equity prices, but instead relate everything to the structure of the forward market in currencies. If we know, for example, that the D Mark is selling at a five percent premium versus the dollar one year out, we should take that knowledge into account in trying to pull out the components of performance of German securities when measured in U.S. dollars. Some interesting publications on this subject will be coming out in the not-too-distant future that will tend to increase our understanding of the whole process by which currency movements affect or don't affect equities.

QUESTION: Staying with the same question but addressing Bill Marshall, you said that your work showed that stock selection added value significantly, but country allocation did not. Could you talk about currencies and whether that added anything to results?

BILL MARSHALL: We really haven't quite refined our attribution modeling to be able to segregate the currency component yet. Some of our managers do sell forward contracts and short currencies where they think that the markets are attractive, but currencies might be weak. Quite honestly, we are unable yet to get our hands on that and measure the true value increment that comes from the currency operations.

However, I side with Gary on the notion that, basically, the currency markets are very efficient. It would take a very high level of technique, of strategy development, I guess, to be able to consistently add value to portfolio results through currency operations. But that's not to say that it can't be done. It's very difficult to prove a negative.

QUESTION: Bill, there has been a series of managers hired to invest internationally and a small number of managers have been fired. Would you comment a bit about your strategy for hiring different kinds of managers? How do you put together a portfolio of international managers for a major plan? What criteria would you use to decide whether a manager should be fired?

BILL MARSHALL: If we go to the discussion about investment manager evaluation, these are what we think of as the four Ps in the business: people, processes, portfolio strategy, and performance. What we like to see is a situation where good people conduct good operations, developing good portfolios with clear rationale, all of which is getting good performance. We think of that as a good basis for hiring managers or retaining them on the team.

In terms of the qualitative aspects, an evidence of weakness might be significant people changes. Just as in a domestic management situation where we see a lot of people movement, this begins to raise a warning flag. Then, as we see changes in the decision-making processes, noses get burned. New techniques are born all the time. We want to make sure that they have some degree of effectiveness. We are always seeking information on new strategies and sometimes it is difficult to develop confidence in them. Where performance has been poor a manager tries something new, and maybe it will work and maybe it won't. It's a qualitative process that we go through, but the bottom line is if we can't sustain enough confidence, and performance simultaneously looks like it's heading downhill on our variance-from-benchmark graphs, then we know what we have to do. So, there is a bit of turnover in managers. It's very expensive to have turnover in the international area, however, because portfolio-to-portfolio transaction costs are much greater than in the United States. What

we really want to do is pick managers with the soundest of fundamentals, and develop the continuing confidence to stay with them through reasonable thick-and-thin.

QUESTION: How do you feel about the fees charged by international managers, Bill? Are they too high, too low, or about right?

BILL MARSHALL: The only way I can comment on that is to say that we do like to put everything on a net-net, bottom-line basis. If we can get a net advantage over our performance index, we're pleased. That's gross performance after subtracting investment management fees, custodial costs, and so forth. Where we find that the prospects of sustaining a net positive advantage over the index are waning, that's when we begin to get uneasy.

QUESTION: What is your net advantage so far? Three percentage points?

BILL MARSHALL: Well, the gross advantage is about 1.4 percent and the investment costs along the way have probably approximated about 100 basis points, so we're at about a 40 basis point net advantage over the index. If we can't get a net advantage over the index, then obviously the message is to go totally passive, which we're somewhat reluctant to do.

QUESTION: Gary indicated in his comments that in the international arena his experience is that domestic U.S. managers are more sophisticated than are the foreign, non-American managers. It's interesting, Bill, that most of your managers are not American. Can you comment on the non-American mix in your manager group as concerns sophistication?

BILL MARSHALL: Basically, the nucleus of our non-U.S. management is in London. We are pleased with what we see in the city of London. They have a long-standing tradition of investment management, augmented now with new techniques coming out of the London Business School. One really fine tool over there is in the form of Data Stream, which facilitates all sorts of screening and modeling and strategy development. We don't see any shortage of sophisticated techniques. It's worked pretty well for us.

QUESTION: Gary, it has been pointed out that if you want to diversify internationally, it would seem to make sense to hire truly international managers that are not permitted to invest in the U.S. What would be the case for hiring global managers who could invest both in the U.S. and outside the U.S., if you're really trying to capture experience in the value of international investing?

GARY BERGSTROM: There are a number of different ways I could address that particular question, depending on the specific circumstances. Obviously, some managers make it simple for you by saying, "We only manage non-U.S. equities." The converse is the difficult issue, when we try to make a judgment about a manager who really likes a global playing field and for one reason or another the program is structured in a more or less compartmentalized fashion, with non-U.S. managers and U.S. managers.

I don't think there are any simple answers. A lot of it, of course, comes down finally to your evaluation of the capability of adding value on the part of the managers. We can show statistically that if a manager has a certain predictive ability—measured by an information coefficient or some sort of formal mathematical technique—and that predictive ability goes beyond a certain level, then generally speaking you should give that person a wider playing field. If that predictive ability remains constant it will lead to better results over the long term. But, very often you get distracted by the practicalities.

QUESTION: What would you say about that, Bill?

BILL MARSHALL: I'd like to echo that. It's all part of getting to know your managers. If your manager really has some significant strengths in the global arena and isn't being utilized in a global context, you're somewhat less than fully engaged; you would be missing out on an opportunity. The key is to monitor the quality of work in the form of an information coefficient or by some other technique that allows you to have confidence that he really can play that game.

QUESTION: Some would argue that non-American managers don't have an ability for investment in the U.S. market that would be comparable to U.S. investment organizations, and therefore non-American investment organizations should not be hired to invest in the U.S. other than on an index basis. What would be your reaction to that?

BILL MARSHALL: I can understand the rationale for the argument, but I'm not sure we totally agree. We have found some evidence of excellent U.S. stock selection being done by managers who are not in the U.S. but who are familiar with it. After all, the U.S. is a very efficient market, and even some of the managers operating within the U.S. have difficulty with it.

No. I don't think there's any particular disadvantage just because you happen to be located in London or somewhere else. That does not say that you cannot select U.S. securities effectively. You need to have developed some effective techniques, but that goes for any other country—Japan, the United Kingdom, Germany, or wherever.

QUESTION: Bill, would you try to quantify management fees, transaction costs, and custodial fees for international investments? Some totaling of what they run, roughly?

BILL MARSHALL: It's a little bit hard to quantify transaction costs, they may be on the order of several percent. In the United Kingdom, for instance, I understand they may be five percent or six percent. In other countries they may be three percent or four percent. I'm not that familiar with it. In terms of portfolio management costs, they have been somewhere in the neighborhood of 70 basis points, given the size of our portfolios.

Custodial costs are quite high, at about 30 basis points. That is because custodianship is both complicated and highly decentralized in the international context, with local sub-custodians holding the securities. For instance, in Japan, securities are held in Japanese custodial accounts but are tied together for us in London in sort of an overall accounting structure, and reported back to us. The communications, teletype, and so forth, needed to sustain that global network is very expensive.

On average, with a 70 basis points management fee, we think of 100 basis points representing the cost of international portfolio management, and if you can get a manager who outperforms the EAFE or global index by more than that, then you are ahead of the game.

QUESTION: Which brings us to international indexing. Gary, would you discuss briefly the pros and cons of international index funds versus active management? And could you also comment on why international indexing hasn't been a big part of this business so far?

GARY BERGSTROM: I think, on the passive-versus-active management issue, if you want the quick answer to why index funds haven't been a big factor yet, just go back to the last four years of data to see that the medians of actively managed international portfolios have generally done better than the passive index over this period of time. If you go back into some earlier periods, that isn't always the case. As the table on relative volatilities shows, international managers as a group have portfolios with higher volatility than the index. In a generally rising period you would expect that they would outperform by some margin. These are some of the practical considerations.

But all that having been said, I wouldn't be terribly surprised if we get into some period in the future, like we have in the United States, where all of a sudden the international index is quite hard to beat over a period of two or three years by active international managers. More or less an international repeat of the cycles we see in the United States. So I wouldn't necessarily be sanguine in just projecting the numbers of the last four years in terms of the relative performance of active management versus passive management. I think a case can be made for both approaches being used in varying percentages in a large program.

QUESTION: Bill, there are two ways that managers can select stocks. One is to first identify a country to invest in and then to look for attractive stocks in that country. Another approach is to look at industries across the world to try to identify attractive companies from the bottom up. Does your experience show that one or the other of these methods is better? Could you comment on those two different approaches and the usefulness of each?

BILL MARSHALL: I'm not really sure that those two different thrusts can be identified as precisely now as we may some day be able to do. Those are two different modes: either the regional or the industrial cut. For the most part, our managers are taking a regional cut. We can certainly tell how well they're selecting within the countries. It's much more difficult, however, to tell how well an industrial cut is working out, although I think that at some point we will be able to get a better handle on it.

International Investing: Setting Objectives, Initiating Operations, and Monitoring Results

David P. Feldman

Other participants have talked about the theory of international investing and the experience of a large pension fund that started its international involvement in the mid-1970s. Our own involvement as active international investors is more recent. We had done an extensive amount of preparatory work and we were about ready to go when consolidation of the Bell System pension funds came along in 1980. We thought that we should take care of first things first, so we put the international move aside. Looking at Bill Marshall's Figure 7 with its double top, I'm moved to say that I'd rather be lucky than smart. Starting in 1982 wasn't too bad from a timing standpoint.

ANOTHER COMPANY'S APPROACH

For the new AT&T, international markets generally are going to be a very important focus in the future. I think these kinds of considerations may have some longer-run bearing on the matter of senior management reluctance to go forward with international investment. The world of business, generally speaking, is becoming much more international. As senior managements become comfortable with that fact, the feeling that "I just don't think that I want to do it," will tend to fade away.

As our own international presence has begun to grow, we have increased the size of our international stake and are now targeting about five percent of our retirement assets, which is right in the middle of the range that Rodger mentioned earlier. Parenthetically, when all is said and done with divestiture, the new AT&T will have about $20 billion in the pension fund. The agreement and arrangements that we have worked out with the regional operating companies are that we will share with them all of the background research we have done on international markets. But, by and large, each of those organizations will be studying its own situation and making its own decisions whether or not to put money abroad.

International will total about one billion dollars of our pension assets over the next five or six years. At first, we'll be moving forward with equities. There are some intriguing elements on the debt side as well, but we like to do things one step after another, and we're going to start with equities.

Program Development Checklist

When you sort out, from the sponsor perspective, an international program and how one goes about it, I think the question of whether one should have such a program at all is in many respects one of the easiest ones to answer. Let me also add at the outset that my remarks are a case study on our own approach. There are a lot of other ways that people have chosen to go at it, and ours was not necessarily the best. Using our experience as a case study is, however, one way of getting at some of the important issues.

After deciding the "if" issue, the next step is to deal with "how?" and after that, "with whom?" The "how" gets into setting your objectives, into really beginning to look long term at what you want to do, and into pulling together an approach that will ensure the long-term success of the program. The long-term aspect of this situation keeps coming up in my remarks because it is very much part-and-parcel of the way to think about it. It's a lot of money and, like the elephant in the tulip patch, you have to be very careful where you put your feet down. Pensions inherently have, or should have in my opinion, a long time horizon, so there need be no rush to judgment in any of these areas.

The "with whom?" matter keeps the pension gossip sheets in business. Manager selection is a very critical part of the implementation. Though it is a part that gets a lot of time and attention, it really comes at the end of a detailed look at the situation.

Setting Objectives

The objective-setting process translated for us into the following specific issues:

- Global or Non-U.S.?
- Stocks or Bonds?
- Active or Passive?
- Country Targets?
- Currency Hedging?
- Lower Volatility,
    Or
    Higher Return?

Another issue that is often overlooked is whether or not the planned commitment of sponsor resources is going to be adequate. Going international is, for most of us, a relatively new venture, and there are some different sets of in-house skills that have to be developed. If you are a sponsor, you need to sort out ahead of time how much do-it-yourself you want to get into. It can be expensive. We have probably the largest base of assets over which to spread that cost, but you still have to think about it. As an aside for those of you who are money managers, one sure way for you not to succeed with us is to come in and say, "It's only a few million dollars. You'll never miss it." I have had people say that. One basis point used to be worth about $6 million

to us. It's going to be down to $2 million when divestiture is completed, but that is still a lot of money.

Risk/Return Assessments and the "Sizing" Issue

After exploring the advantages of international investing, our conclusion was that it is possible, at least looking retrospectively, to get the best of both worlds: to reduce risk, and to improve return. The future remains to be seen, but if you take a look in the rear-view mirror, it is encouraging. In Figure 1, various combinations of the S&P and EAFE investments are plotted for 10-year periods. Without exception, while the slope of the curve may vary from period to period, the addition of international assets, over all 10-year periods, did lead to a reduction of risk, and, generally speaking, an improvement in return.

Taking the theoretical or the academic approach and translating it into a management approach is something that really constitutes the heart of the sponsor staff's job. One of the issues that concerned us most about our international program and one we spent considerable time thinking through was the sizing/timing question: how much and how soon? In addition, there are questions about what happens when you look at a real portfolio as opposed to a paper one,

FIGURE 1
Frank Russell international long-term: increased return and reduced risk

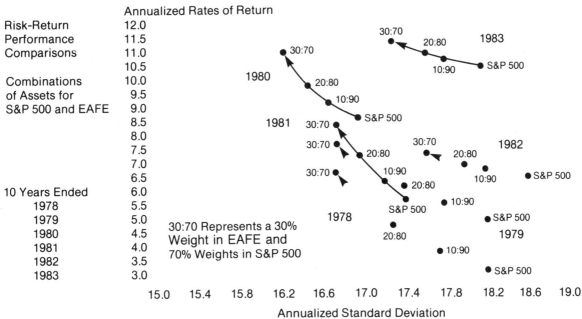

and there are some particular issues in international diversification. Finally, the market inefficiencies come into play. I think that the sponsor needs to get a handle for his own situation, and to tailor the results of the international program that he adopts. This means that everyone is going to do it a little bit differently. In our own case, when we looked at the sizing decision, the research that we had available to us indicated that on a theoretical basis you should probably hold a very substantial portion of your portfolio in non-U.S. assets in order to insure that you have a theoretically efficient portfolio. Some work we looked at suggested that since the markets are roughly equivalent in size, and the U.S. market is 50 percent of the total capitalization and non-U.S. the other 50 percent, perhaps an optimum point might lie at 50 percent non-domestic. From a practical standpoint going from zero to 50 percent with any amount of money is managerially unworkable. You would certainly get resistance at the Board level if you proposed something like that. In our case, we decided to begin with a very small percentage, five percent, and see the results.

The pension decision process is a long-term

one, and there's plenty of time to fine-tune it as we go along. Given that first cut—five percent, plus or minus—as our target, we came out with a couple of interesting implications. The studies that we looked at of optimal portfolios with percentage constraints indicated that immediate and simultaneous exposure to all the markets wasn't really required. When we were down in the lower percentage of assets, the EAFE curve didn't differ substantially from the Japan-alone curve, for example, from a risk reduction standpoint (Figure 2). It appears that there are no penalties in the low end of the spectrum for incomplete diversification. The conclusion that we drew from this was not to be unduly concerned over the country issue at the outset. We worried about everything, but this is not really a critical decision in the early stages.

The real portfolio effect is a question that we don't have the answer to. Intuitively, we know that there are interactions with the other pension assets. But it is not immediately clear how the optimal proportion of these securities might change if one fund had 15 percent in real property (or whether the ideal country weightings also differed). The asset mix question has

FIGURE 2

Risk reduction from international investments (10 year period ending Dec. 1983)

Percent of S&P 500's Standard Deviation

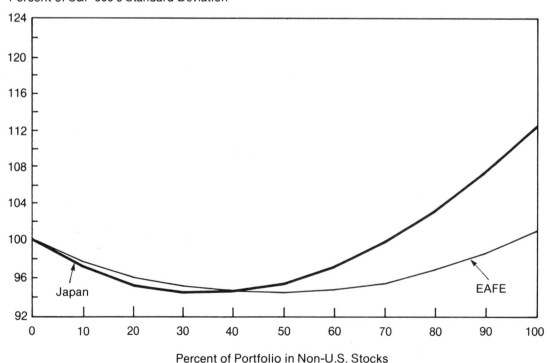

Percent of Portfolio in Non-U.S. Stocks

become very complicated these days. We haven't seen or been able to accomplish a lot of good research on how all assets interact. I suspect it is a very difficult analytical problem. What it suggests to us is to keep in mind that there are likely to be some interactions. Move forward cautiously; take a step at a time; don't base all of your decisions on a portfolio mix that does not, in fact, pertain to the real world.

The research does indicate that there is significant risk reduction with assets from relatively few international markets. That suggests that some of the managers may not track the EAFE Index exactly, but if you have reasonably continuous representation in Japan and the key Common Market countries, you will get most of the diversification that you are looking for.

When you are down in the low end of the range with respect to international assets as a percent of total assets, below 10 percent, you are about in line with the consensus (see Figure 3). Nobody is willing to go beyond 10 percent. Below 10 percent there's not a lot of difference in risk reduction. That led us to conclude that we might therefore worry a good bit less about diversification per se, and focus a good bit more on enhanc-

ing the returns that we get as we move into international investment. I can also suggest that benchmark measuring can be overdone. We like to measure things, but at low levels. It may or may not provide meaningful results.

Active/Passive Considerations

Finally, in terms of market efficiency, the research is relatively inconclusive. There is some evidence that national markets may be efficient internally, and less so across markets. The conclusion we drew from this set of concerns and issues was that we would go active rather than passive, at least at the outset. I should hasten to add that passive management is alive and well at AT&T. We have been long-standing proponents of passive management for the domestic markets. We have roughly 10 percent of our total assets, and 20 to 25 percent of the equity, being managed passively. About $1.5 billion is in our internally run passive fund. It has been very effective for us.

When we looked at the international side, however, we came to a different conclusion. There is a limited but rapidly growing number

FIGURE 3

Risk reduction from international investments (10 Year period ending Dec. 1983)

Percent of S&P 500's Standard Deviation

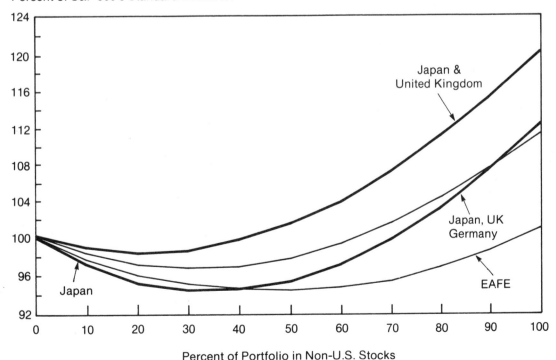

Percent of Portfolio in Non-U.S. Stocks

of active non-U.S. portfolios at the moment. We felt this made comparisons with the EAFE Index somewhat tenuous. The theory would suggest that efficiency requires a lot of knowledgeable investors. It cuts two ways. If there isn't a critical mass, you worry a little bit about the effectiveness of a passive strategy. It also suggests that there may well be opportunities for extra return among and across markets.

The index itself is another problem. We had to work with the S&P 500 for a long time before we began to sort out its various difficulties. When we did, we substantially expanded our domestic index fund to include non-S&P issues, to capture some of the small capitalization effect. But EAFE is newer, and there may well be some problems there.

The other element in our decision is the idea that there may well be something extra in the countries themselves in terms of return. Globally, some countries, over the very long run, seem to have a low tendency towards chronic inflation. Certainly there is a potential for higher productivity and growth. Operating from a lower base, their central banks have been able to keep money supply and deficits under better control than we have. So, we think there is a possibility in some markets that is intrinsically advantageous for return availability.

Ground Rules, Standards, and Manager Selection

Summing all of those factors together, we established what might be called a pilot program. I guess 5 percent of a $20 billion fund is a good-sized pilot. The starting point was to select a diversified group of active managers. The basic ground rule was non-U.S portfolios, and that was a very pragmatic, non-theoretical issue on our part. We were just getting started. We had a very broad base of U.S. assets, and we wanted to begin to factor in some of the diversification effect. What we were looking for was more international assets, so we picked non-U.S. portfolios.

The managers have country-selection freedom and can hedge currencies as part of their investment approach. We do not allow currency speculation. They do have discretion as to whether they are in cash or stocks and they do not have to be fully invested. Our initial criteria for manager selection were these: non-U.S.

global, equity orientation; separate account experience; SEC registered; and active management-oriented. That gave us something like 75, or some such unwieldy number. After we had pared that list down and finally selected the group we would go out and meet, we were faced with a very basic objective issue: How specific should we be in terms of studying performance benchmarks? As I said, the numbers tend to feed themselves. There were several problems for us in setting a specific benchmark target. One, as I mentioned, was that we weren't really sure of the effectiveness of the index. Second, we were particularly concerned that if we said you have to do two percent better than EAFE, and it turned out to be too easy, we would get discrimination among the managers. Equally, on the other side, if you make the target too tough, I think it is human nature to begin to generate a short-run orientation. We didn't want to do that, either.

Other folks may go at it differently, but our conclusion was to tell the managers to be themselves, just to do the best they could. We will remain the judge as to whether that is sufficient or not over a fair, full market cycle. Manager selection remains an art rather than a science. We try to bring all the numbers to bear that we can, but the most important thing as we went through this process and tried to set objectives for managers was first to sort out what each did and what each one's basic approach was, and then to monitor in an ongoing way to determine whether or not they were maintaining a consistent approach. It has been our feeling—and our experience—that almost any reasonable, well-thought-out approach will work over a period of time if it is maintained. Hop around a lot and you are going to make the wrong jump at the wrong time. So, we look for consistency.

We started out with 75 manager possibilities, 66 of whom returned the questionnaires. This was a fair amount of work in itself. Our first set of criteria was met by 32. We took a closer look at 20, using the above criteria. Again, I should reiterate that this is not a static. The 20 happened to be a cut at that point in time. We have continued to evaluate new managers as they come on the scene. It's a very rapidly growing area and we are very reluctant to shut the door to anyone. In terms of where we are going in the future, the cut didn't mean that the people we looked at were in and the rest were out. We continue to talk to the people who didn't make that first cut, as well as to the manager world at large. It is very much a living process that must be kept up with on a day-to-day basis.

The other element that we tried to bring into play was the issue of style and diversification. We want managers who will do very well over time and managers whose style variations will tend to cancel out. From the questionnaires, the interviews, and talking with our consultants, we came up with a way of categorizing people. Maybe it wasn't the best way, but it was convenient for us. The aim, as we went forward, was to spread our money across all the categories, following the oldest investment adage of all in terms of not putting all of our eggs in one basket.

In our categorization scheme we identified four types of managers. We saw a *diversified manager* as one with core holdings in the major areas of the world, trying to combine top-down and bottom-up approaches with a centralized portfolio management process at its headquarters. A *concentrated manager* was one that tended to make more significant country bets than the others. There were fewer *value managers*, those with a bottom-up approach with overall stress on individual company selection. We also identified a *currency manager* category, where people didn't manage on that basis completely but did take a more active view of the currency question in their investment decisions.

SUMMARY

We have hired some managers, and we will hire additional managers as we go forward. To date we are pleased with the results of the program. The greater knowledge of the individual management processes that we're getting as we meet with managers and get some hands-on experience is very valuable. We have a long-term commitment and, hopefully, we'll learn and grow together. Our fondest hope and expectation is that we'll prosper together in this enterprise.

International Investing: Monitoring Manager and Program Results

Jan Twardowski

International investing has come a long way from the dark days of the FAF conferences of the early 1980s when the subject was lumped on a panel with all the "funnies"—you know, precious metals, Picassos, pork bellies, and Japan. One year it wasn't even on the program—not one word about international investing. Meanwhile, U.S. pension funds had invested about $5 billion overseas and Japan was up 50 percent. But we have our own seminars now and international investment has arrived; it is now in the mainstream and can no longer be ignored. Our investments are paying off.

Bill Marshall and Dave Feldman set the stage, explaining, how large sponsors by way of very thorough processes, select international investment managers and set objectives, both for the program as a whole and for the individual managers. We can now move on to the matter of monitoring program results.

First of all, keep in mind that currently, the mainstream of international investing for U.S. institutions is non-U.S. equity investing, mostly by active managers. There is little passive management as yet. Suppose that a sponsor has launched an international investment program involving five percent of total pension assets. I think it's fair to call that a pilot program, a learning process. Nevertheless, you must keep track of it effectively. How do you do that, monitoring not just the rates of return on the international investments but monitoring the whole process, including the benefits to your total investment plan?

THE MONITORING PROCESS

The problem is a bit complicated. You have all the complexities of measuring U.S. investment results in each of the 20 or more countries that you may be investing in worldwide, plus an overlay of fluctuating currencies. So there is a good reason for this complication, and please forgive the poor measurer for the complexities of the basic process! To assist in the explanation, I've broken my presentation into sections that treat the various aspects separately.

Aspects of the Process

First, we will discuss the purposes and methods of monitoring international portfolios, establish criteria for the necessary measurements, and review some actual results from the last few years. We will show that managers have indeed added value against measurement criteria. Then we're going to look at some techniques for identifying the sources of achieved rates of return—how they did it, not just what they did—where the managers added the value. Then I will describe the details of the portfolio management process. It's quite different internationally than for managing assets within just one country. We will see how different firms follow different approaches and use different tactics. Then we'll get to the key issue: What has been the actual impact of international equity investing on the U.S. equity portfolio? Again, we have some actual numbers to help with that. I'll close with a comment about the future. I believe that non-U.S. investing is only the start. True world-wide investing is the future.

While numbers are an important part of monitoring, it is still useful to keep in mind the importance of qualitative assessments. The numbers can help us understand the managers, but it is people who produce the results. We still have to go back to the essential issue, which is identifying the good people, and that's a qualitative process.

Monitoring Purposes and Methods

The first purpose of a monitoring program is to measure the success of the international program as a whole—in other words, to measure the decision of the sponsor to go international. I might add that this is one area where the sponsors, especially sponsors of the large pension funds, are actually leading their investment managers in making what some think of as a fairly radical decision to place some assets offshore. The objectives are, I think, perfectly clear for everyone:

to lower the risk and raise the return for the plan's total equity portfolio.

Next, we want to assess each manager's achievements. To do this we use the Capital International Europe, Australia, and Far East Index, affectionately known as EAFE. We all have problems with it, but it is the best index available. It's our passive non-U.S. equity standard. A better active-management standard would be a group of discretionary accounts managed under similar objectives, a "peer group performance universe." We now have over 150 portfolios in such a universe, very comparable and very useful for comparing results. So, we don't just have indexes; we also have actual portfolios.

Some Recent Results

Now for some results. To keep it simple, let's concentrate on the last three years when most of the U.S. pension money moved overseas. We have a good, representative sample of thirty-seven portfolios managed by eighteen firms, all with a full three-year performance history. Figure 1 shows quartile graphs for periods ending at the close of 1983. The EAFE Index, which is adjusted for withholding taxes here, is in the fourth quartile for each of the periods. So, the managers have added value over a passive approach throughout this period. Incidentally, the performance of Japanese equities over the period probably had a lot to do with this outcome. It is instructive to see that the international managers produced a margin of perhaps four percent over the index. Also note that the range from best to worst is quite wide, but that the quartiles are fairly close. Most of the funds are concentrated close to the medians.

Just to make sure that results aren't dominated by a single year, compare the individual years in Figure 2. We see something similar, with the median beating the index in each year. Most

FIGURE 1
Universe quartile ranges (Non-US equity portfolios)

Annual Rates of Return

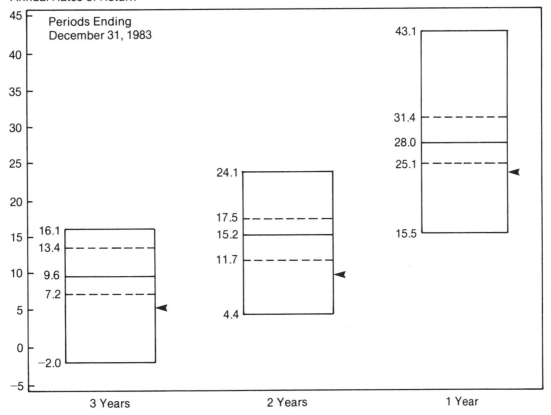

◄ EAFE Index, Adjusted for Withholding Taxes

FIGURE 2
Universe quartile ranges (Non-US equity portfolios)
Annual Rates of Return

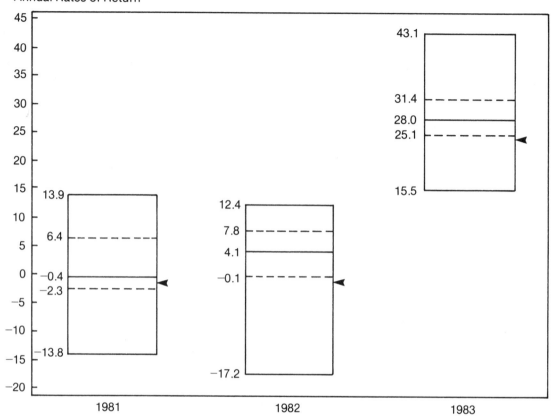

◄ EAFE Index, Adjusted for Withholding Taxes

of the excess return occurred in 1982 and 1983. Again, the quartiles are fairly close. Notice particularly the median 1983 figure of 28 percent, which compares favorably with the S&P return of about 22.5 percent. In spite of the dollar's strength, 1983 was an excellent year for international investing.

As background, we should remember that this three-year period presented a rather difficult environment for investing internationally. Both Bill Marshall and Gary Bergstrom alluded to this, and the reason was almost solely the strength in the U.S. dollar. If you look at the markets in local currency terms alone, as shown in Table 1, you can see that the EAFE Index —that's all the markets in EAFE weighted together but measured in local currencies alone—beat the S&P by six percentage points per year. Japan, the United Kingdom, and Germany—the three largest in the EAFE index, together representing 70 percent of

the total index weight—each beat the S&P by a substantial margin in local currency terms. However, when you convert them to dollars to add the currency effect, only Japan beat the S&P and then only marginally. The currency impact, large over this period, is shown on the right-hand side. On average, 11 percent per year was lost on currency conversion. The dollar's strength was a difficult hurdle to overcome. Whether that sort

TABLE 1. A difficult environment (3 years ended December 1983)

	Local currency	US dollars	Currency impact
S&P 500	12%	12%	
EAFE Index	18	7	(11)
Japan	18	13	(5)
United Kingdom	24	5	(19)
Germany	22	9	(13)

of trend will continue or perhaps reverse is an open question.

Sources of Return

The managers have added value. But how? There's general agreement that it is useful to break the results into parts, as is done in Table 2. Keep in mind that this shows *contributions* to returns, not returns. The first four columns of numbers add up to the total return on the right. The Table features sample managers A and B and a composite of the two for a pension fund, with two international managers compared to the EAFE Index. These are actual numbers from real managers, both first quartile firms for this period.

Taking each column in order, in the first we put the currency effect, which leaves the other three columns (country selection, stock selection and cash/bond allocation) in local currency terms. The second column measures the impact of the managers' and the index's weightings in the markets, showing how they would have performed if they had simply invested passively in each market. The result can be called country selection when it is compared with the index. The third column, stock selection, compares the equity return within each country against the local Index.

The fourth column is cash/bond allocation. Nearly all of the portfolio managers have the freedom to use cash and bonds—dollar cash, non-dollar cash and, usually, non-dollar bonds—as equity substitutes, keeping in mind that the EAFE bogey is a 100 percent equity index. They're permitted to, say, buy D Mark bonds or yen CDs if they think such assets are appropriate as equity alternatives. Such a decision could be an opportunity cost or a benefit when measured against each local market.

These two managers are quite different, except in the area of currency management, where both exceeded the index because of their dollar reserves. But, in country selection, manager B lost over 5 percentage points while manager A nearly matched the Index. In stock selection both managers had a positive, very substantial effect from picking good stocks in the various countries. The Index benchmark's contribution, of course, is zero. Manager B was also able to use his positions in fixed interest securities quite positively, as shown in the cash/bond column.

For manager A, currency and stock selection were positive contributors, versus the Index. Manager B did well against the index in all areas but country selection. These numbers can all be calculated from fairly simple formulas, and there are no residuals if the input data is accurate. When you actually go through the process, there are other things to look for as well. You'll want to know the individual country breakdown for each of the four measurement areas, for example, to see in which countries and when the positive selection occurred. The system you use should provide that level of detail if you are to monitor effectively.

Next, we will divide this three-year period into two 18-month periods, because the markets moved differently in each. The first period (Figure 3) runs from January 1981 through June 1982, the second (Figure 4) from July 1982 through December 1983. These two graphs are on the same scale, so they can be compared directly. The first period is one of fairly moderate market movements. There was not a great deal of change, but the currency element was quite painful and very difficult to overcome for all managers. While the Index was down about 16 percent, most managers were able to moderate that loss somewhat through the use of dollar cash holdings.

Moving to the second period shown in Figure 4, we see quite a different story. This was a time of booming markets worldwide, not just in the United States. The currency was negative but not really very important, being far overshadowed by the country selection aspect. Notice, that *all*

TABLE 2. Summary table: Contributions to returns (3 years ended December 31, 1983)

	Currency	Country selection	Stock selection	Cash/bond allocation	Total return
Manager A	(9.0)%	19.7%	3.1%	.6%	14.4%
Manager B	(7.4)	14.2	6.0	2.8	15.6
Composite	(8.2)	16.9	4.5	1.7	15.0
EAFE Index	(12.9)	19.9	—	—	7.0

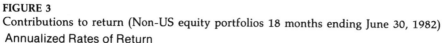

FIGURE 3

Contributions to return (Non-US equity portfolios 18 months ending June 30, 1982)
Annualized Rates of Return

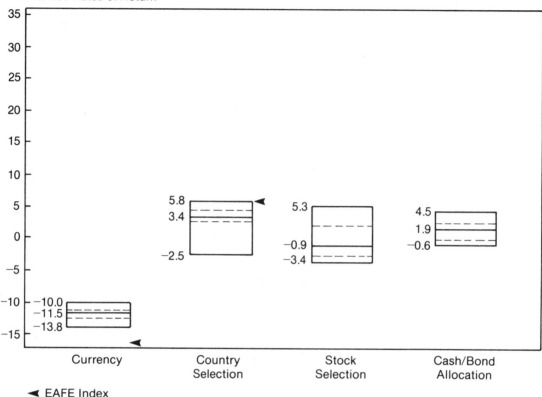

◄ EAFE Index

of the stock selection numbers are positive, showing that all managers in the universe had positive stock selection. It's not only important to know what the managers were doing against the index, but also what they were doing versus everyone else. The reason for the positive stock selection here is primarily Japan, the largest country in the index. The stocks that non-Japanese investors generally buy in Japan are not the stocks that make up the greatest part of the index. They tend to be high-tech companies, and the so-called "foreigner favorites," which did extremely well. All you had to do was own them and you had a good stock selection number for Japan.

Manager Approaches

Moving away from quantitative assessment, how do different managers manage their portfolios? We've seen some of the return results, but that's not really adequate for judgments. How do they differ? When we started consulting internation-

ally in the mid-1970s, all we had to go on was what the managers told us about the way they managed money. As we all know, what someone tells you can differ remarkably from what actually happens, not out of a desire to obfuscate, but just from communication problems. I remember a 1979 meeting with a London-based manager who described his current market position as bullish because he had built up a 75 percent position in equities. Later that week, another manager said he was extremely cautions about the market and had raised a 25 percent cash position. Clearly, we need some common denominators.

What we really want to know is how the portfolios are actually managed. Figure 5 is an "activity profile." It is known affectionately by some clients as a target, definitely not for shooting at managers but maybe for shooting at consultants. We're trying to describe levels of activity, and measure the kinds of "bets" that the managers make. Any point toward the center of the circle is more passive, less active, and more

FIGURE 4
Contributions to return (Non-US equity portfolios 18 months ending December 31, 1983)

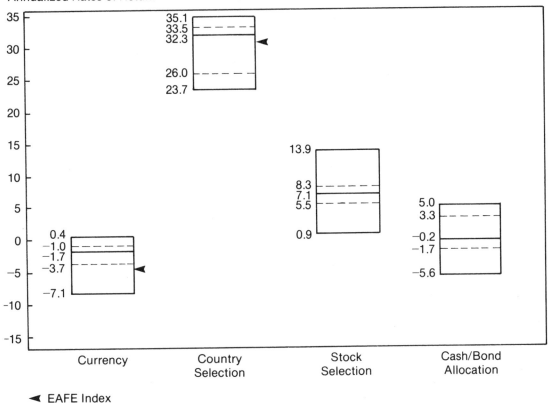

Annualized Rates of Return

◄ EAFE Index

like the index. At the outer fringes—the ends of the arrows—you would have a much more aggressive, active posture. The circle is divided into thirds: country allocation, cash/bond (or non-equity) allocation, and equity concentration.

In the *country allocation* area, we consider two aspects of the country bets: weighting and activity. Japan is about 45 percent of the EAFE Index. In the weighting section, we see how willing a manager is to make bets away from that norm. Is he willing to move only in a tight range of 40 percent to 50 percent? Or, is he much more aggressive, willing to go down to 20 percent at some times and up to 70 percent at other times? We measure that by looking at the actual portfolio movements over time. The dotted circular line going through the middle is the median of all the portfolios we measure. Returning to our two managers, A and B, we've made this an easy example to read because manager A is far more

FIGURE 5
Activity profile

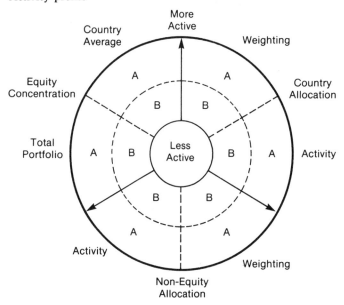

aggressive (toward the outer edge) in all categories than manager B.

In the second part of the country allocation section we look at activity, or the rapidity with which the country allocation bets can be changed. A high figure could be achieved by a single change in the Japanese weighting from 70 to 20 or by very rapid movements from 40 to 50, or 40 to 45.

In the cash/bond, non-equity allocation area it's the same concept: How large a bet, how large a weighting, and how much activity?

Equity concentration is simply a measure of the R^2 of the portfolios against the appropriate indexes. In the center—toward the less active core—we would see a high R^2, low concentrations and high diversification. More aggressive portfolios would lie out toward the fringes, with a lower R^2 and more concentrations of stocks different from the Indexes. Part of the equity concentration measures the average R^2 for all countries in the portfolio, while the other part measures the R^2 of the total portfolio.

Remember that what we're trying to understand is how managers differ in their portfolio techniques. Our managers A and B are obviously quite different. In reality it is much more complicated. Some managers might be very aggressive in the country bets but use little cash. Others might have concentrated portfolios, or their activity in moving around the countries might be very high, while they hold relatively diversified portfolios within the countries. All of these differences can be illustrated via the activity profile. It's another way of getting at that style question which Dave Feldman alluded to.

It is important to remember throughout this complex quantitative analysis that these are just tools for trying to understand the managers better. We need to avoid 20/20 hindsight, or "backwards jobbing" as they call it in London. It's easy to look back and say "Why did (or didn't) you do that?" But it's the managers who know how to run the portfolios, not the sponsors or consultants. All we're trying to do is gain a better understanding of their techniques.

Effect on U.S. Equity Portfolios

Now let's turn to the crucial question: What has been the effect of international investing on the U.S. equity portfolio's return and risk? To get at this, we will look at actual results for 10 U.S. pension funds which for a full 3 years have invested substantial assets in international equities. The average invested abroad over the period for these 10 funds was about 10 percent. In Figure 6, what we'd like to see of course is arrows pointing toward the upper left, moving the U.S. equity portfolio toward reduced risk and increased return.

Looking at the arrows for the individual years, we see that in 1981 these funds achieved a slight return enhancement and a substantial risk reduction. 1982 was a year of negative return contribution (mostly due to currency effects), but still recorded a fairly substantial risk reduction. 1983 was positive on both counts. For three-year totals, these 10 funds' overseas investments did not raise their returns, but the risk reduction effect—about 6 percent—was important. That's not bad, considering that the amount of international investment was only about 10 percent of total assets during this period. So, international investment was a good diversifier of the U.S. equity portfolios. The actual risk reduction effect was even stronger than theory would have predicted.

Rodger Smith showed some similar numbers, too. The theory definitely worked on the risk side, and we can probably project that into the future. It has worked again recently on the return side, too. Over the three-year period we had a "self-supporting learning experience".

Table 3 shows the actual return and risk data for all 10 pension funds. I want to call your atten-

FIGURE 6
Effect of international investing on US equity return and risk

Return

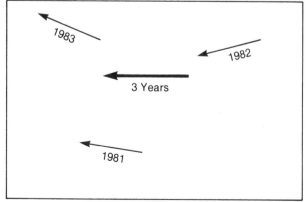

Risk

tion to Fund 5. All of these held only non-U.S. equities international portfolios, except Fund 5. It's return is quite different because it is the only world portfolio in the set: That is, it is the only one where the client decided to go with a world objective rather than just a non-U.S. one, permitting the manager to hold U.S. stocks as well as non-U.S. That strategy certainly paid off in the period under review.

Last, many other useful analytics can be done in the monitoring/ measurement area. Figure 7 is an example looking at Japanese portfolios, comparing P/E ratios versus market capitalizations. Each of the dots represents a portfolio of a money management firm in Japan, either a separate Japanese portfolio or the Japanese segment of an international portfolio. It shows quite a range between low-cap and high-cap, and low-P/E and

TABLE 3. Impact on US equity portfolios (36 month period ending 12/31/83)

	Return				Risk (standard deviation)		
	US	International	Combined		US	International	Combined
Fund 1	13.6	12.7	13.5		14.0	14.3	12.9
Fund 2	15.3	12.9	14.8		13.4	15.3	12.4
Fund 3	12.8	12.0	12.7		13.6	15.4	13.5
Fund 4	14.1	11.9	13.8		20.1	16.4	18.2
Fund 5	10.8	24.7	12.8		17.9	12.4	16.7
Fund 6	10.1	10.7	10.0		17.5	14.7	15.9
Fund 7	11.0	5.7	10.6		13.9	14.7	13.3
Fund 8	12.8	11.3	12.8		14.8	15.3	14.0
Fund 9	12.8	10.3	12.3		15.9	15.0	15.1
Fund 10	14.6	8.2	14.3		14.0	14.8	13.5

FIGURE 7
Japan portfolio characteristics (capitalization size—P/E ratio June 30, 1983)

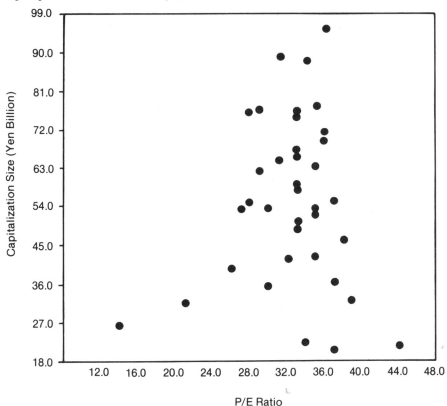

high-P/E postures. The first thing you notice is how expensive Japan is in P/E terms. Then you see that in the large-cap issues there's very little variation to P/E ratio. Most of the managers fall within a small range. It broadens out as we drop down into the smaller companies, and there we see some quite different strategies being pursued by those firms along the bottom. The two at the lower left are firms with strategies which are quite different from the others. They are examples of the value-oriented firms that are so rare in the business. You can see that what they do matches what they say, at least in Japan.

LOOKING AHEAD

Our firm has a portfolio accounting system which tracks about $35 billion of U.S. "domestic" equity portfolios. In a recently completed survey, we found that in these supposedly all-U.S. portfolios about 2 percent—or $700 million—is actually invested in non-U.S. issues. Interesting names are creeping into U.S. managers' portfolios. The long-awaited move is afoot.

To close, I'd like to go back to the "world versus non-U.S." issue. The reality right now is that most pension funds separate U.S. equity investing from non-U.S. equity investing, not an unreasonable position given the skills of the managers and the thinking of most sponsors. But we, as a firm, believe that the future lies in worldwide investing with both U.S. and international assets combined under one manager. The logic is strong. There's a growing demand for worldwide stock pickers and researchers, people who can differentiate easily among Hewlett-Packard, Hitachi, and Olivetti or among SmithKline, Glaxo, and Yamanouchi. It's no longer possible for analysts to ignore their industries' competitors outside the United States, or for portfolio managers to ignore the securities outside their own country. We think that sponsors will expect their managers to take a worldwide perspective in a few more years. The competition is heating up!

Feldman/Twardowski Q & A Session

MODERATOR: Dave, what period of time will you use to measure the results of your managers? When and how would you decide to fire one?

DAVE FELDMAN: We would have at least three to five years of experience, particularly in a start-up phase like this. We have, historically, tried to bend over backwards to be sure that a situation couldn't be fixed before we terminated a manager. You have to avoid the rearview-mirror syndrome that Jan just talked about. We try very hard not to focus inordinately on performance numbers. At the same time, somewhere down the road the results have to turn out reasonably favorably, in three to five years initially. Firings on the international side are something that we really haven't gotten into. We're working on the hiring side right now.

QUESTION: If a manager has two years of really bad results, is he out the door?

DAVE FELDMAN: No.

QUESTION: O.K. Jan, are you really as powerful in the work you do with sponsoring corporations as many managers believe?

JAN TWARDOWSKI: Probably not. A consultant just gives advice. We don't make the decisions for clients. We measure, and we look at the qualitative side to provide extra information on managers. We're providing pension sponsors with information that they would look for themselves. It's a make-or-buy decision for most clients. We're not smarter than they or the managers are, and we certainly don't know the "right way" to manage money internationally. It's simply a process of gathering information and providing it to the sponsors as they need it. There's a myth that consultants put out "fire so-and-so" bulletins, and all the clients do so in lock-step. It just doesn't happen. First of all, termination recommendations are rare (trigger-happy treasurers are more common) and second, the clients don't go along like puppies. They are fairly strong-minded corporate executives with their own ideas.

QUESTION: As a follow-up, do you tell your clients specifically which managers to hire and which managers not to hire?

JAN TWARDOWSKI: Like all consultants, we'll provide a "recommended" list of firms to fill a particular role for a particular client. Clients have very different ideas about how to pursue any investment goal, including international investing. They have different needs and preferences. Some want to hire firms with local nationals on the scene doing their own research in the Far East; some are more value-oriented. So we try to find firms which fit those usually quite reasonable preferences and come up with a recommended list.

QUESTION: Dave, you indicate that you use four style categories. One of those is a currency-management orientation. Its been observed that it's very hard to add value with currencies, and a lot of people ignore that in the long run. It's therefore interesting to see that as one of your four style categories. Would you comment on that a little, and on the number of managers you see that are able to add value with currency bets?

DAVE FELDMAN: We didn't go at the classification process on the basis of neatly dividing up the world of managers. As somebody has already pointed out, on the value side, for example, there are relatively few people who do that. At the same time, when we went through our own analysis, in looking at investment processes and how managers went about it, there were some who spent more time and effort looking at the currency situation and reacting to that. That is what we tried to capture under that category. There weren't a lot of firms there, either. And there are gray areas in all of this. As Jan says, you sort through and try to find out how they go about the investment process, and there are some where the currency decision is a bigger element in their approach than it is in others. That's all it really means.

QUESTION: Jan, one of Dave's charts showed there wasn't much difference in risk reduction for an investment in the EAFE Index vis-à-vis

Japan only, for relatively small commitments of up to 10 percent. If that's true, then why wouldn't you go for the higher performance you'd expect in Japan and recommend that your clients hire managers that specialized just in investing in Japan or the Far East, as opposed to more on an international scale?

JAN TWARDOWSKI: Some people go to the racetrack and bet on the favorite every time—but there are lots of other horses out there and betting the favorite might not be a winning strategy in the long run. The Japanese market is volatile, it's high-priced, and there are other places to invest. In the same way that we think it's not prudent to limit your investments to the United States, why would it be prudent to limit your investments to Japan and the United States? Sure, Japan has had a good record so far, and it may do well in the future, but hindsight is *not* a viable investment strategy. There are other markets, and individual stocks in other markets, which will also do well. Why ignore them? The managers have demonstrated skills in finding opportunities in all parts of the world, not just in Japan and the Far East.

QUESTION: Dave, do you want to comment on that a little bit, about going for regional specialty managers as opposed to "international managers, non-U.S."?

DAVE FELDMAN: Yes, I think that's another area where you separate the theory from the practice. What we saw suggested to us that one could focus on the value-added side of the investment equation without worrying inordinately in trying to balance out the diversification side. That was not intended to suggest that as a viable strategy, you would just go into Japan. It comes back to "don't put all your eggs in one basket." You are looking back at what has happened. I think all you can draw from that is that a relatively inexperienced sponsor doesn't have to worry about diversification as much as he might have thought initially.

QUESTION: Can either of you elaborate on the discussion we've had about the EAFE Index and the problems of using EAFE as a real index and a benchmark? What about the composition of the index, the shortcomings it has, and the possible alternatives to getting a better index?

JAN TWARDOWSKI: Very quickly, it just doesn't have enough stocks, basically, in the markets it covers. It's oriented toward large-capitalization stocks. In each market there is usually a better "native" index, if I may use that term: The Financial Times–Actuaries (FTA) in London, the FAZ in Germany, the Tokyo Stock Exchange Index. But, for the most comprehensive worldwide data, the EAFE Index is still the best. I understand that Capital International is working on some of its defects and may well remedy them. While there's a lot of talk about its shortcomings, the EAFE is still a good index, overall.

QUESTION: There's a lot of discussion in the U.S. about ways a corporation should structure its portfolio managers. Are there core international managers and non-core managers? What would be the categories that you would suggest a plan sponsor use to categorize international managers?

JAN TWARDOWSKI: We're a little leery about putting names on things and setting up style categories. We quite rightly get shot at by managers when we take it too far. It is possible to categorize some managers as core managers if that means they tend to be well diversified. There are a few low-P/E, value-oriented managers. Otherwise, the nuances can be rather small and difficult to identify with names. It's really a matter of understanding how each individual firm manages its portfolios.

DAVE FELDMAN: The objective here—the reason for even setting something up—is to try to measure consistency of approach. What you call them, or the various categories you use, is considerably less important, because you get into enormous gray areas and you can spend a lot of unproductive time just arguing among yourselves or with the managers as to what category or what style they are. It's more an analytical approach to measure the degree of consistency over time than it is to say that one is this or one is that.

QUESTION: Dave, you're going to invest roughly a billion dollars outside the United States. How many managers is the optimal number for that?

DAVE FELDMAN: I don't think there is any optimum. From our viewpoint, managers today can certainly handle accounts of $100 million. We have not gone that high as yet. One of the questions we will be considering as we move forward with the program is the extent to which you add managers versus adding additional cash to those already selected. Having just worked our way down from more than 100 manager candidates, we have no desire to replicate that situation.

QUESTION: So you would look for good managers first and then try to put together a package of managers that would make sense in an overall international structure, rather than come about the process the other way, which is set up as a structure and they try to find managers that fit into the structure?

DAVE FELDMAN: Yes, very much so. It's a process. The people change, the approach changes, and we learn more as we go forward. You try to leave room to add a new manager or a new approach if it seems appropriate.

QUESTION: Jan, could you quickly tell us how you differentiate the currency effect from the country effect in measuring contributions to return?

JAN TWARDOWSKI: There's a fairly simple formula for that. You just take out the currency element for each month, that's the heart of it.

QUESTION: Is currency hedging easy to take into account when measuring performance?

JAN TWARDOWSKI: If you have the data on the different hedges that have been used and if you have correct market values at the end of each month, which are difficult for some custodians to provide, then it's quite easy to do. The calculation is not difficult, given the necessary data inputs.

International Investing: Global Investment Research/Management (I)

David I. Fisher

I would like to take two different cuts at the question of international research. The first is an organizational cut—what an organization must know and do in order to be able to make intelligent investment decisions on a global basis. The second cut is a look at the individual analyst and some of the complications that he runs into in doing research outside the United States—what the differences are in looking at companies in different markets.

BASIC PRINCIPLES

Let me begin by sharing with you some principles that are basic to my thought process about international investment. If you have trouble accepting the principles, you are going to have even more trouble coping with the opinions that follow. These principles are:

- There is no one simple solution to the investment business.
- Superior knowledge makes a positive difference
- The investment process should be a partnership between research and portfolio management.
- You should invest in a security because you believe it represents good value, not on the hope that someone else will be willing to pay more for it later.
- The world does not neatly divide into U.S. and non-U.S. components.
- Analysts that follow the competition in a global industry on a worldwide basis will make better investment decisions than those who only follow the companies domiciled in a single country.
- Organizations that know more about non-U.S. companies, economies, and markets will be better investors inside the United States as a result of that knowledge. Conversely, investment decisions outside the United States will benefit materially from superior insights into U.S. companies, the U.S. economy, and U.S. securities markets.

- Investment organizations should strive for a diversity of people in terms of background, interests, political biases, and analytical approaches. The one value they should share is integrity.

Let me repeat that these principles are basic to everything that follows, and I believe them with a passion.

INDUSTRY ANALYSIS: AN EXAMPLE

When I started in this business almost 17 years ago, it was as a consumer electronics analyst. Interestingly, the questions that one had to try to get the answers to haven't changed much in 17 years and they are essentially the same questions that an analyst needs to consider for a number of other global industries.

What did one need to know 17 years ago to do the consumer electronics industry?

The Demand Element

First, we need to know where a company's orders are coming from. The questions are fairly obvious.

- What are the determinants of demand?
- What are the economic factors that most influence demand? Do they vary by country?
- What about demographics? What influence do they have and how do they differ by country?
- Are new-product introductions or product improvements important influences on the level of demand?
- How long does the product tend to last and to what extent can its replacement cycle be influenced?

In the late sixties the answers to these questions went as follows. Demand for consumer electronics tended to correlate best with disposable personal income. People in total seemed to spend a relatively stable percentage of their disposable personal income on consumer electronics products; the occasions on which consumers have been willing to spend more are linked to major new product introductions. Examples would be the record player, television, and color television. Since the days that I was following the industry, the video tape recorder and the personal computer have been examples of products that substantially increased the percentage of income that people are willing to spend on consumer electronics products. It was fair to say then and is still accurate today that products did not tend to wear out, but rather were replaced because new products were introduced that had noticeably improved features—e.g., color replaced black and white television, stereo replaced monaural records, larger screen and portable television were developed—all were changes that stimulated demand.

The Supply Element

On the supply side of the equation are also a number of questions that need to be asked and answered:

- How capital intensive is the business?
- How labor intensive is the business?
- How much flexibility is there in increasing or decreasing supply?
- To what extent must the supply be designed for a specific national market?
- Is the technology such that getting new entrants into the business would be difficult?
- What other factors are at work that might influence supply?

As in the case of demand, the answers to these questions have not changed a great deal. Supply is not capital intensive, but is labor intensive. A well-disciplined labor force can quickly be brought up to speed to produce new consumer electronics products. The necessary technology is available to a number of industry participants. Especially in television, there are specific differences in the technical requirements for specific national markets. There is not, therefore, complete international interchangeability.

Strategic/Competitive Information

Beyond the basic elements of supply and demand, other company-oriented information was needed, including for example:

- Distribution systems—global and national
- The role of OEM business
- The importance of market share
- Brand name recognition
- Manufacturing driven versus marketing driven orientation
- Breadth of product line
- Level of vertical integration both in marketing and manufacturing

Differentiating between Companies

To contrast one company with another and to make choices between companies, it is important to learn about their philosophies, as well as about their methods.

- Motivation of management—what are they trying to accomplish and why? What is the definition of success? What is the reward system? Where does this business fit within the total scheme of a company's activities?
- Profitability—how profitable is this business for the company?
- Investment in facilities, technology, and distribution—how does it compare to other company business areas? To other companies?
- Impact of currency—what currency is the raw material priced in? What currency is the final product priced in?

What I have identified so far is a Mother, God, and Country list of things about which analysts of a global industry should strive to know. The reality is that the analyst will never know everything about everything. At a minimum, however, the analyst ought to be able to identify those things that he or she doesn't know the answer to. For example, it is quite possible that the analyst can't figure out what motivates management or how they define success. To the extent that they haven't been able to figure this out, it could certainly influence the conviction that one has on the investment decision.

SPECIAL CONSIDERATIONS: A JAPANESE EXAMPLE

Now I would like to take a different cut at the global research process. What I have said so far implies that there is a research methodology that can be applied to global industries no matter in what countries the companies may be based. I strongly believe that to be the case. At the same time, be aware that there are major differences that exist between countries and economies. Because what we do is not research for the sake of research, but research toward the end of making better investment decisions, it is important to identify some of the special considerations that apply to individual markets. Now let's look at some of these considerations via a contrast between the United States and Japan.

Reporting and Information Flow Differences

Japan differs from the United States in a number of important respects:

- Earnings are generally announced semiannually—not quarterly.
- Companies will break sales down by major product line, but tend to say little about profitability.
- Companies, concurrently with earnings announcements, make forecasts for the subsequent 6 and 12 months. These forecasts tend to be meaningfully below what the company really expects.
- Most companies don't have a professional investor capability.
- Getting a broad exposure to the functional management of a Japanese company is difficult.
- The time available in an interview tends to be less. If you also have a language problem, it becomes a lot less.
- The job of the analyst at brokerage firms tends to be a pass-through job. Analysts seldom have the time or opportunity to be truly knowledgeable.

Valuation of Securities

Once the needed information is available, there are differences in major valuation elements in setting prices.

- There is more focus on recurring profits than on EPS.
- The percentage change in recurring profits tends to be more important than the P/E ratio.
- Parent company earnings receive more attention from investors than do consolidated earnings.

Management Philosophy and Other Environmental Differences

Management philosophy is the area in which Japanese business decisions tend to have a longer-term horizon. The best example of this may have been the willingness of Japanese companies to absorb large losses in the semiconductor industry in the early 1970s. Consensus decision making tends to result in a longer time to make a decision and a shorter time to implement it. The concept of lifetime employment means that companies need to be more flexible in being able to move from one product line to another. "If we can't employ people making radios, we'd better figure out what other product line we can turn to for employment of the labor to which we are obligated." There is a comfortableness with a much higher level of financial leverage, owing to the interrelationship between the industrial concern and the lender.

There are identifiable differences between U.S. and Japanese theory and methods of accounting in areas such as the consolidation of subsidiaries, the reporting of profit on installment sales, the use of special reserves, inventory accounting, and pension accounting. There is, however, something even more basic to understand than any one of these factors, the impact of which can vary considerably by industry. This one key conceptual difference between accounting in the United States and accounting in Japan is probably responsible, in turn, for 90 percent of the differences in accounting theory between the two countries.

In Japan, the system of accounting and financial reporting is really a tax compliance system. In short, an overriding purpose of the financial statements is to serve as a base for reporting to tax authorities. Tax policy is, therefore, a driving force in the formation of accounting policy. Deductions may not be taken for tax purposes unless they are actually reported on the books.

By contrast, in the United States there is no direct theoretical link between the tax returns and the financial statements. It follows from this, of course, that one will never see a deferred income tax credit or debit in Japanese financial statements. There is no need to tax-effect the difference, since there is virtually no difference in the first place. This direct relationship of financial reporting and the taxing system does introduce an element of conservativism into Japanese accounting.

There is an obvious tendency to reduce income, to the extent possible, in order to minimize the tax liability. Nevertheless, this is only a tendency and does not hold true in every case.

Market and Investor Differences

What are some of the stock selection considerations that are relatively unique to Japan? First, individuals account for over 60 percent of the transactions there, so it is more of a retail market than in the United States. An exemption from capital gains taxes on the first 49 trades in a given year tends to encourage this. Parent company earnings receive more focus than consolidated earnings. The market has tended to sell at a high P/E by world standards for many years.

Changes in recurring profits are more focused upon than changes in earnings per share, and the percentage change is often more important than the absolute level. Gratis shares are regularly used to increase, in effect, dividends to the shareholders. At the same time, Japanese stock charts are often not adjusted for gratis issues. Short-term fads and rumors can be exceptionally important in setting short-term prices. The influence of the broker is more predominant, by far, than in the U.S. market. There is an active convertible market which, for some reason, is often inefficiently priced. Put another way, it is not unusual to find convertibles priced at or below conversion parity and with a higher yield.

The Capital Advantage

As in any market, the professional investor must figure out what his competitive advantage is. In Japan, it certainly is not that we will be the first to hear the latest rumor and be able to act accordingly. We have found that we can really add value by bringing a long-term and global perspective to a price-setting environment that tends to be local and short-term. I might add that the successful implementation of this strategy requires conviction about the companies selected, a willingness to treat short-term price action as an opportunity rather than as a threat and, finally, patience.

BRINGING THE PIECES TOGETHER

So far, what we have dealt with are some principles; some ideas on how to go about the process of global industry research, and some of the things to think about when you look at an individual country. The question that remains is how all this gets brought together. Should one expect all of this information to reside in one individual: the global industry analyst? Is there any alternative? My view is that it is reasonable to expect all of this information to reside within an *organization*, but probably unreasonable to think that any one individual will have all of the answers. Therefore, it follows that the challenge is to figure out how to ensure an environment in which the combination of industry and individual market insights are available to the total organization. In my view, that takes hard work, a division of labor, mutual respect among the participants in the process, and time working together so that there is a real opportunity to calibrate the individual strengths, weaknesses, and even the biases.

I said at the outset that there isn't a single solution to the investment process. I have presented an approach that has met with some success in our organization. It says that global perspective is important, but that it must be combined with local expertise. While not explicitly stated, my remarks also imply that one ought not be dependent on external sources. In any short-term period they can be helpful but, with all due respect to many people in the business for whom I have a lot of personal admiration, I really believe that a major investment organization has to begin with the notion of self-sufficiency. That is particularly true in an era of great change in many countries—the kind of change we are likely to see over the next few years. In this kind of environment, it is a good feeling to be able to depend on internal associates with whom you have worked for many years rather than on external sources which, for reasons beyond your control, may be here today and gone tomorrow.

In summary, doing global research is not easy, but it is *critical* to long-term success. It is also absolutely necessary to be sensitive to the differences between markets. It should not be expected that one individual will be the fountain of all wisdom as it relates to both a global industry and all the nuances of a specific market—but it is reasonable to expect that this wisdom will reside within a single organization and be utilized effectively in the decision-making process.

International Investing: Global Investment Research/Management (II)

Karl Van Horn

In considering worldwide financial analysis—or international investment research—there is a key investment issue. Both from the standpoint of a global investment manager and from the point of view of his client, that key investment issue is *investment technology*. Investment technology, a conveniently vague term, is the application of quantitative techniques to the extended global marketplace.

NEEDED: A DISCIPLINED INVESTMENT APPROACH

A disciplined investment approach is even more critical in a multimarket environment than in single-market investing. You must have a more disciplined approach internationally because of the staggering amount of choices that the manager has to make. The tools of modern portfolio theory are just beginning to be applied internationally to complement the manager's intuitive insights. Domestically, this marriage of investment technology and intuitive judgment started about 15 years ago.

Joining Investment Technology and Human Judgment

There are two aspects of this mutually supportive relationship between investment technology and human judgment. First is the marshalling of the research inputs. This is essential to support the investment process in a manner consistent with the manager's style. Just five years ago, let alone in 1974 when ERISA opened the door to international diversification, the trick was simply to produce the information. Almost any input was better than nothing. Most comparative analysis was about country growth rates.

Newly-minted investment researchers, wherever they worked, reported that they were among the first financial analysts to visit major continental European countries, and almost certainly the first non-locals to make those visits. Comparative industry research just didn't exist.

A typical stock selection question was not whether Philips was more attractive than Siemens, but whether Philips was a better buy than Unilever.

Today, the truth is that the international investment world is in danger of suffocating in a flood of data. Any portfolio manager/analyst with a decent supply of soft dollars to hand out or a fat internal budget can choose to be inundated with high-quality material from every continent—or he can dump fast and accurate data bases into a PC on his own desk. British brokers, for example, who have opened offices in Tokyo and New York, publish comparisons between European, American, and Japanese electrical companies based upon the classic blend of shoe leather and spreadsheet analysis. The portfolio manager/analyst can pull off Reuters or Telerate everything he can possible need—from the outlook for Dutch bonds, to what the German Chancellor said 15 minutes before, to information about the Australian budget. The trouble is, at least 98 percent of that information is just so much white noise.

The *ability to sift information* is now the name of the game. I'm talking about getting rid of the gravel so you can see the gold gleaming at the bottom of the pan, and then getting those nuggets into the client's portfolio fast. But how many international investment firms are there, where the investment research function essentially operates in a different information orbit from the people who structure the client portfolios? Unfortunately, the answer is: quite a few.

Today's reality is that too much effort is spent generating even more information. Tomorrow's priorities should be the application of investment technology to the analysis of the information that is already available. Those of you who have had an opportunity to look at a number of international portfolios have noticed, perhaps with the increasing sense of the frustration suggested by Jan Twardowski, a certain vanilla ice cream similarity. My own feeling is that a lot of international investment managers haven't yet begun to apply the quantitative technology required to help human beings formulate distinctive flavors of portfolio style.

Therefore, the first aspect of a mutually supportive relationship between investment technology and human judgment revolves around the marshalling of research inputs. I thought David Fisher addressed this issue extremely effectively.

What is the second aspect of this mutually supportive relationship? It is the control of portfolios for tomorrow's optimal return, and the identification of the elements of skill and chance in yesterday's portfolio results. But how many international managers can simulate the impact on the total portfolio of a significant rise in English technology stocks? Or, how many international managers can accurately pinpoint why they outperformed the benchmark? Unfortunately, the answer is: not many.

We have recently seen the emergence of international services that can analyze the components of portfolio performance for the client, weeks or months after the fact. This is useful information when rating managers, but it is considerably less helpful to the manager himself. The manager must have this information daily if he is to make optimum use of it. I've said that tomorrow's number one international manager and client challenge will be the application of investment technology to the extended global marketplace. In saying that, I'm using the high beam out front rather than looking at the lights in the rearview mirror.

The need then is to link the emerging investment technology with human judgment, in a global context. This involves using technology first to capture the key information inputs and then to integrate these inputs into the investment process. With a bit of luck, the international manager's results would then be achieved in a manner consistent with the style he describes in his glossy marketing brochure. I'm sure there must be some quantitative buzzword to describe this linkage. At least some research directors would have portfolio managers—and consultants, and clients— believe that the approach to investment analysis should determine a firm's style. I think those people are looking through the wrong end of the telescope. It seems to me that a global investment firm's first step should be to identify how it can add value to a client's portfolio. In other words, where do its own skills really lie? Then, and only then, can you formulate the correct approach and implement it in a coherent way. Research should be a means to an end, not an end in itself.

IMPROVING THE ODDS ON WINNING

So how—in today's, let alone tomorrow's, global investment Olympics—can a given manager improve his chances of being on the plus side of a game that nets out to zero? I just can't get out of my mind one of John Maynard Keynes' three principles for successful investing: "A careful selection of a few investments, held steadfastly in fairly large units through thick and thin, perhaps for several years." That doesn't sound much like the current rotational dog's breakfast between markets and within markets. What Keynes was really getting at was leaving the reinvestment risk to somebody else. Obviously, that presumes that your initial judgments were generally correct on a country, a currency, an industry, or a company.

Changing Success Parameters

But are longer-term fundamental judgments in a multimarket universe best made by financial analysts in a traditional way? Probably not. We all know that an international manager is looking at an interrelated yet interdependent group of decisions. What market—Italy, Spain, or neither? What currency—the DM or the Guilder? What type of asset—don't we know that "bond" is no longer a four-letter word for equity jockeys? Which names—Toshiba or Canon? These decisions, no matter how messy, split along two lines—macro and micro. First, the macrodimensions, which are country economic comparisons, market valuations, currencies, and so on. Ten years ago, the trick was to identify the fast-growing industrialized countries and simply pour the money in. Today, I really doubt whether international investing based on relative country secular growth rates has much of a role to play. Japan is no longer growing five times as fast as Europe and two and a half times quicker than the United States. You could throw a blanket over the future relative growth rates of the industrialized countries of the Northern Hemisphere. I see no need to allocate expensive information resources to grind out extensive tables on individual country GNPs.

But what about the fast growers in Southeast Asia or in the Third World? The answer is probably yes, on a selective basis. The judgment there is sociopolitical, not economic/financial. The data sources would be the IMF and the World Bank, not DRI, Wharton, or an in-house economist.

I also doubt whether much effort should be directed toward timing different national markets. Capital flows between the world's major countries and even some of the smaller ones is resulting in greater intermarket efficiencies. Where extremes in a country's valuation relative to the rest of the world occur, that extreme is now more often for sociopolitical reasons. Recent examples are Bob Hawkes' Australia, Mitterand's France, China's Hong Kong, and Craxi's Italy. As with macroeconomic country research, moneymaking bellringers are more likely to come from the political scientist than from the traditional economist.

The same sort of input reappraisal also applies to currency. How many economists got the dollar right recently, or often enough for their clients to make real money? Not many. It seems as if one day the players are emphasizing real exchange rates and the next day they are looking at interest rate differentials. Right now everybody's talking about budget deficits and the election. Most international managers today somehow combine currency picks with market picks in one decision. It reminds me of the famous cross-legged trapeze artist. I'm convinced that currency judgments can add value only if the currency decision is made entirely separately from the market decision. There is simply nothing quite like concentrating on one thing at a time. You can, on an exceptions basis, pick up returns from currency hedging, particularly through cross-hedges. Some people made spectacular gains through hedging sterling into yen in late 1982. The research input required was found on the Reuters screen and in the London *Economist*. How many of you remember the classic story of Sherlock Holmes' best friend? Holmes' brilliant insight was that the dog didn't bark in the night. For equity investors, the dog that doesn't bark can be all the asset categories that are not in an equity index. Bonds are a prime example. I am not talking about the day-to-day, in-and-out sloshing of funds between cash, bonds, stocks, and pork bellies. What I am talking about is active management to beat a passive equity benchmark.

For instance, in Germany there are only about 450 quoted industrial companies. A number of them are completely illiquid. German equity prices are driven by movements in the bond market. But hold the phone: The way to over-weight German equities is not only to stock up with DM bonds. Most often, the DM and German interest rates move in tandem within a spread. Dutch state bonds are highly liquid and suffer no withholding taxes. Substituting Dutch bonds for German equities is a judgment call based upon interpreting information off a screen. What you must have is experience, not a Fujitsu number-cruncher. The legendary in-house one-armed economist probably won't be much help either.

Adding Value through New Approaches

It should come as no surprise that in my view tomorrow's macroeconomic research theme will be that value is added through having the right people in front of the right screens with the right data on those screens. Like David Fisher, I question the need for in-house gurus. Soft dollars can buy a whole range of economic expertise. Today's information technology can process and package that expertise at a cost which has fallen dramatically. What I'm saying is that you can buy a floppy disk for a lot less than you have to pay for a Harvard M.B.A. or a London Business School M.B.A.

Internationally, macrodecisions, are already a plateful. But you also have to make microdecisions. What about industry and stock selection? Should the black-box route go international? Emphatically not, in my opinion. Plenty of inefficiencies remain for intuitive, well-informed Homo sapiens to dig out. The issue, again, is information technology—getting the right information to informed decision makers with minimal slippage. Where could a global investment firm get that information on the most cost-effective basis? My own experience tells me that the international roles of the traditional financial analyst and of the firm's large internal research capability are hovering today just about where they were domestically 15 years ago. Heightened competitive distinctions between management styles, the introduction of investment technology and a glut of information are forcing a real transformation to smaller units with unique skills.

Every firm will increasingly have to answer the following question: Is it more cost-effective to source in-house or outside? It is certainly possible now to do either one internationally. It was difficult until recently to get the right kind of data into machine-usable form and do it in a timely way. I'm convinced that the PC explosion and the rapid growth of global brokers will soon change this. Major investment management firms will insist that brokers provide subjective security rankings and supportive evidence, such as earnings estimates, on an IBM-compatible floppy disk. Soft dollars will pay for soft copy. Written reports and phone calls will be done on a by-exception basis. Key personnel will once again have that great luxury, the time to create.

Everybody in this room is familiar with the kind of computer screens that can be run on domestic U.S. securities. The same kind of arraying possibilities are beginning to emerge for non-U.S. securities, notably in the United Kingdom and Japan. Currently available data base management software permits the arranging of the data backwards, upside, downside, sideways, or inside-out, and then using it to drive a color plotter. Does this mean that black-box portfolios should be the end product? Again, No! No! No! No! Leveraging valuable people with experience is the objective. I mean freeing people to apply their intuitive skills to choosing individual holdings, without doing vast amounts of manual screening.

One of my colleagues many years ago, for example, spent a week going through the little yellow cards then used in the United Kingdom called Extel cards. These Extel cards held a lot of good, solid corporate data. My colleague was looking for small-cap, high-growth electrical companies to investigate in greater detail. Investigation in greater detail is still a must, but the screen would now take five or ten minutes instead of a week.

Furthermore, it is now possible to make industry bets on a worldwide basis. Choosing sunrise sectors or picking survivors in the sunset sectors are examples. I know firsthand that this kind of research can add significant value. It means linking industrial themes across national borders. To me, pursuing such an approach should be done with external resources. Brokers are probably not the best sources available. Three days at the Hanover Fair in Germany with an industrial consultant, or one afternoon in Tokyo with a consumer electronics specialist, can offer unique insights in a time-efficient way. Of course, a consultant's

background data should be in the portfolio manager/analyst's data base.

What's Ahead in Leveraging People

Let's assume that you give me the benefit of the doubt and agree that the route to go is generally external. Information technologies offer the best way to handle the inputs. What then is the next step? Let's delve into the future, and I'm really talking about the "just around the corner" future. Having tracked the relevant information in soft, on-line form, the second stage of people leverage is an "expert system" to arrange that information. Expert systems specialize in particular problems. In a sense, they simply massage data in a sophisticated way to pick out subtle patterns and relationships. Expert systems are different from data base tools. Expert systems can learn from an expert user. A skilled portfolio manager/analyst could tell such a system, for example, to dredge up a group of French consumer stocks that have various qualities. When the names flash on the screen, the manager/analyst may, for example, say to his PC, "No, dummy, Moet-Chandon was too exposed to the Iranian consumer market. And also, would you please talk to our trading PC about the liquidity in Club Med stock?" The charm of that approach is that it offers a lot of flexibility on stock selection, but at the same time it pinpoints a manageable range of options. There is absolutely nothing passive about it. The analyst/portfolio manager imposes his judgment and intuitive skills on the selection process, but he does so in minimum time.

Closing the Loop: Portfolio Control and Review

All this stream of consciousness about marshalling research inputs may have erased from your memory bank the other end of the investment process. I'm referring to portfolio control and review. It's now time to close the loop. There are really two considerations here. The buzzwords are: *ex ante* and *ex post*, or "what was expected?" and "what happened?" In my experience, larger ERISA plans—such as GTE and American Telephone and their consultants, such as the Frank Russell Company—are starting to make the same *ex ante* requests internationally that they do domestically. They are beginning to want a controlled ride. You know the approach. The plan sponsor says, "You were hired to be aggressive. I don't really care how you do it, as long as your R^2 is under 0.7, the beta is 1.8, and you don't closet-index in Japan." Those kinds of marching orders tell me more than just how I'm expected to run the money. The message is also that I need to know an awful lot about the characteristics of the individual holdings and their impact on the total portfolio. If I put five percent of the portfolio into a Japanese technology stock, what does that do for the R^2? If I don't hold the U.K. oil sector, or Siemens in Germany, what does that tell me about residual risk? Most international managers don't realize that the answer is: plenty! The manager needs quantitative tools to make such *ex ante* analyses. These tools are spun off the kind of data-fed decision process we were talking about a few moments ago. The tools I'm talking about are more or less available off the shelf. The problem is, most managers are psyched out and put off from applying them from sheer fear of being caught with their pants down.

Of equal importance is *ex post* analysis, otherwise known as portfolio review. What happened *after* you made all those good, well-analyzed decisions? How much of the performance came from stock selection? Did that bold move into Dutch bonds pay off? Did the sunrise sector in Japan outperform some industrial version of Lazarus in the United Kingdom? The *ex post* tools to answer questions like that are less well developed than the *ex ante* tools. But you've got to

have competence with both tools to manage money in the multimarket world of the 1980s.

I really believe in international portfolio review and control. That's not simply out of curiosity or out of the desire to create rationalizations for past investment performance. It's infinitely more difficult to chart a future investment course if a manager can't read the dials in his own portfolio. What we're really talking about is knowing in detail the quantitative impact of current over- and under-weightings in individual stocks. The manager also has to know whether he is making or losing money, and how much, on his country, currency and industry bets. If a manager can't do this, a prudent investment style produces vanilla ice cream and an aggressive style produces speculation.

CONCLUSION

By now, perhaps you have noticed that I haven't addressed any of the specific items such as comparative P/Es and company visits. I hope that hasn't been too painful. Over the past ten years, international investing has become an integral part of a growing number of ERISA plans. During the next ten years, investment technology will become an integral part of the global investment train. It will begin with the client cow-catcher at the front of the locomotive. It will end with the portfolio-review lantern at the end of the caboose.

Fisher/Van Horn Q & A Session

MODERATOR: There are obviously some major implications in what Karl just said, both for investment management organizations in the international business as well as for the brokerage firms that provide them with information. Karl had, as I was listening, quite a different perspective and cut on how to do research on a global basis than David did. I'd like to start by asking David if he would react to the view that investment technology is coming to global research in the way that Karl suggests.

DAVID FISHER: I think there's a lot of truth in what Karl was suggesting, especially when he puts it in terms of freeing up people to spend more time thinking creatively about answers. There are several aspects of it. One is that which Karl described. I think the other is more like the focus of our own efforts, and that is to figure out how the technology helps us to communicate internally, because when you're dealing with investment people in seven different offices and many time zones, the ability to have the insights and opinions on an immediate basis is really the key. So our effort with the technology would be geared more to how we would internalize it. Clearly, there are two challenges. One is the screening kind of mechanism that Karl referred to. The other is the communications side.

QUESTION: David, could you talk a bit about the industries that you feel lend themselves to global research and the industries that don't?

DAVID FISHER: Consumer electronics, chemicals, energy, autos, electrical equipment, steel, metals, drugs, and transportation are some that do lend themselves. Others that I don't think do are utilities, which tend to be more of a function of the local environment, and probably not retailing. I'm sure I've missed a bunch.

QUESTION: What about financial?

DAVID FISHER: Let me answer that this way: I think on the financial side you can almost reverse what I said before. In most cases, you have global analysts responsible and then local consultants that provide input and advice. On the financial side, you have local people responsible and global analysts that consult, because there are some overlaps.

QUESTION: Karl, are you saying that you really don't want to be confused by talking to management? All you really want to do is talk to the floppy disk? Management is going to hype the company, so don't get confused by talking with them?

KARL VAN HORN: No, I'm not suggesting that. What I am suggesting is that insights, particularly into globalized industries such as David referred to, given the pace of technological change and international integration, more likely can be found in the insights of industrial consultants, whose training and sole mission in life is providing observations on their particular area of expertise. What you're really interested in is whether Toshiba's product is going to do better than Canon's or Motorola's or Philips' product. What you can get off a screen is whether or not the financials are such that they will support that type of strategic, corporate, or specific product development.

QUESTION: What kind of organizations do these industrial consultants work in? I assume they don't work in the brokerage firms that we now commonly employ.

KARL VAN HORN: That's a very interesting question. As you'll remember, back in the late 1960s and early 1970s in this country, the leading brokerage firms often went out into the industrial sector and hired individuals who were in the chemical industry, or in the drug industry, or working for IBM and brought them in as, in effect, industrial consultants who were backstopped by analytical paramedics as far as the data appraisal was concerned. So there are precedents for this marriage between industrial insights and financial judgments within the brokerage community in the United States. It does not exist, however, internationally. So the type of firm that you would go to would be like Arthur D. Little or Batelle, or perhaps some disgruntled member of the Kyocera Research Department in Kyoto who is now working out of his own home, providing consultancy to industry and to people like ourselves.

QUESTION: David, could you talk a little bit more about how you get your information, particularly about how important direct company contact is in the context of information gathering and research?

DAVID FISHER: It is important in two ways. One is using the industrial consultants that Karl refers to, except we call them analysts. Those are the people we hire, and we try to get them next to people that have that kind of industrial experience. We really believe that doing research over time, calling on companies with the same individuals from our organization, makes a difference, and that's what we try to do. Our leg up isn't the ability to call on more companies; our leg up is to be able to look back over 15 years and say we've had the same individuals calling on these 150 companies outside the United States. And we've translated that from the need to get on an airplane and fly off to wherever they are to the ability to pick up the telephone and talk to them in Japan, Germany, the United Kingdom, Canada, or the United States, and to interview an individual with whom we have developed a relationship over time. So our view is that having miles—what Karl referred to as experience—in this business is important. Making a lot of dumb mistakes, which I certainly have done, is something that you'll learn from. Having the people out there is good, by itself, but it's also important in terms of the quality of information you'll get back.

QUESTION: Karl, you make the point properly that one of the problems in the business is that there is too much information, an overflow of information. You've pointed out some kinds of information that aren't required, like country growth rates in the industrial countries and so on. Could you give a more complete list of the information that is not required, particularly the kinds that are widely available but not useful? Then could you also talk, on the other side, about what information *is* needed? What is the right data, and is it only financial data that you need?

KARL VAN HORN: Let me begin with what is not needed. At the macrolevel, I suggested that what is not needed is 20 different single point estimates for Japanese GNP. At the microlevel, what is not needed is 100 reports on Hitachi by Morgan Stanley, Nomura, Nikko, Yamaichi, Daiwa, Vickers da Costa, and so forth. Now, what inputs do you need? At the macrolevel you need information that relates to the economic and financial dynamics of what I've referred to as the selected countries in the Southern Hemisphere. You're really going to be making judgments about Singapore, Malaysia, Taiwan, South Korea, and so forth.

QUESTION: That's things like real growth rate, and political stability?

KARL VAN HORN: Yes, and demographics—how many people are under 20 years of age and the rest of it. The classic sort of thing that some of the old goats like David and I used to do in Europe 20 years ago. I'm sure David could have told you what percentage of the Dutch population was under 30 years of age in 1962. That was a very important input in determining what Philips' earnings would be. That's the sort of information you're after.

Then, at the corporate or microlevel, I think you're really interested in evaluating relative corporate strategies and whether they're being followed through on. That's the sort of role that I would foresee for an industrial consultant. With respect to the financial analysis, there is enough information around so that you can tell whether there are any shenanigans going on with the numbers. That comes from experience. It's much like looking at a painting in a museum. If, as David said, you've made enough mistakes and seen enough pictures, you'll know which one is a good one or a bad one. You just want to determine that the company isn't going bankrupt and that there's a good chance it can finance its corporate strategy. You can do so very easily from existing public data now. You don't have to go see the company.

QUESTION: David, you talked from the base of an organization that has $20 billion under management and 50 or 60 analysts. Could you talk a little bit about the critical mass of manpower necessary to run an international research strategy and, if you aren't large enough to have that kind of resource available, then what would you suggest to an investment organization in terms of research?

DAVID FISHER: I'm not sure what the critical mass really is. I say that honestly. We got there over time; there's more than 25 years of history in it, and I can tell you with some conviction that 10 years ago we didn't have the critical mass and today we do. But I'm not sure what the in-between answer is.

QUESTION: Is it five or maybe ten analysts?

DAVID FISHER: I guess what I really believe is that it is more a mentality than it is a number. It is a mentality that begins to think about things in a different way, that begins to examine inputs and tries to bring things together. When Distillers in the United Kingdom announces the acquisition of its Johnny Walker distributor in the United States, which has been owned by Esmark, the ability to have some perspective both on Esmark and on Distillers becomes a very important matter. I guess that if I were a smaller organization—if I were consulting to a smaller organization that didn't manage international assets and yet saw some value in all this—I would start by getting people to read the *Financial Times*. Then I would find out who within the organization really found it to be interesting. Then I'd divide the world up into geographic areas and say, "O.K., *you* keep us informed on those things going on in Japan that relate to our U.S. investment decisions, and *you* keep us informed on those things going on in Europe that relate to our U.S. investment decisions, etc." I'd go through that sort of thing and let it build. When we established our office in Geneva in 1962, it was for no other reason than to help us make U.S. investment decisions. I'm not suggesting that you have to have an office in Geneva or someplace else to do it. I think I'd just try and do it gradually.

QUESTION: If you are an investment organization, that would be a key message. If you believe that the domestic markets are going to be more internationalized over the next five years, which I think most all of us do, and now you're running just domestic money and you're trying to figure out how you start this going without big costs, here's clearly a way to do it. Karl, can you add to that?

KARL VAN HORN: It's not a question of quantity. It's a question of quality. Which would you prefer to have: a group of ten people each with an average experience level in international investment matters of ten years, or 100 people each with one year of international investment experience? It amounts to the same thing, 100 man-years.

QUESTION: I've got two other questions that I'd like to ask. One for Karl is: how do you develop a relevant data base on a global basis when the fundamental assumptions used to generate the numbers vary a great deal from country to country? How long does it take to develop this kind of data base, and are there some data bases available now that can be used for this purpose?

KARL VAN HORN: Yes, there are some available in the United Kingdom and in Japan, although they are selective. In a more comprehensive fashion, the time frame probably is two to five years for widespread availability. I think we'll be surprised and find the time frame will be compressed, simply because of the efforts of the brokerage community around the world to provide enhanced services to their clients.

QUESTION: One last question for David: When you are analyzing a global industry and you've got companies in Country A and Country B and Country C, and they each have different accounting practices, is the right strategy to homogenize those practices all to a U.S. standard and then analyze? Or, is the right strategy to look at each individual country so that you can make individual country comparisons, Japan versus Japan, United Kingdom versus United Kingdom, and so on?

DAVID FISHER: I think that the answer is the latter, not the former. Somehow, it's easy to have the notion that what we do in the United States is right because we do it. Let me tell you, that doesn't make it right, and that particularly applies to accounting standards. I think one ought to understand the differences between the U.S. accounting treatment and British and Japanese and the Continent, but I think it's a mistake to try to convert them to one standard. If you must have a standard, I could have a long argument with you on why that standard ought not to be U.S. accounting.

Global Investment Portfolios: The United Kingdom and Scandinavia

Michael W. R. Dobson

I would like to look at the key factors we focus on in managing global equity portfolios and how the emphasis we give to these factors differs from market to market and from time to time. To illustrate, I will use the U.K. and Scandinavian markets as examples of what we highlight when looking at very distinct investment areas. As we see it, the three decisions in international equity management are the country or market decision, the stock decision, and the currency decision. We believe that the long-run key to out-performance lies in the decisions on which country (which market) you are going to be invested in and on which stocks you buy within that market. Therefore, our process *generally* places equal emphasis on those two key decision areas.

INVESTING ACROSS MARKETS

Taking Local Characteristics into Account

I say *generally* because I think it's essential to be flexible in your approach, to be prepared to adapt your style to the different characteristics you find between markets, and to the different stages in the economic and equity market cycles. This flexibility is not a sign of uncertainty or vagueness as to investment style or philosophy, but simply a recognition that markets are not stagnant. The driving forces behind international markets are constantly evolving. Part of this, of course, is because we're talking about immature, inefficient markets, where the key parameters are changing. So, a successful international manager's style must be capable of evolution too.

The United Kingdom and Scandinavian markets are two obvious examples of markets having very different characteristics. The Scandinavian markets are essentially two-tier markets where a few large multinational companies with little dependence on the local market or economy account for a large percentage of the markets' total capitalization. In Sweden, for example, over 30 percent of the market's capitalization is accounted for by companies that account for less than 15 percent of domestic market sales. Therefore, we seek to invest in four or five outstanding companies irrespective of whether they're located in Sweden, Denmark, or Norway. These are typically companies in the electronics and health-care fields that really must be analyzed on a global basis. The direct impact of the Swedish economy on an Astra, a Pharmacia, or even an Ericsson is quite limited. Similarly, changes in the Danish or Norwegian economies are of little importance to a Novo or an STK.

As to the larger markets, where we generally place equal emphasis on market and stock selection, on the macro- and microaspects, we think that our process must be adaptable to different stages in the market cycle. In the United Kingdom we are nearing the end of a seven-year bull market. We are at the stage where stock selection is becoming increasingly important, as opposed to a few years ago, where the key was simply to have a substantial U.K. weighting in your portfolio to take advantage of a broad advance in the indexes from an oversold position.

I would argue that this will increasingly be the pattern for most international markets during 1984. After 18 months or so of very strong performance we are at the stage where stock selection skills are becoming increasingly important. In order to make real money, it's not good enough now to buy the indexes. The economic fundamentals in many markets may look right, but it's increasingly difficult to find exciting undervalued situations.

To sum up our broad style, notwithstanding our different approaches to different markets and our varied emphases at different stages in the market cycle, we place equal weights on market and stock selection. Overall, we believe that you should not overemphasize one against the other, which would shut you off from one major area of potential return.

Emphasis to Shift in Future

In the future, however, the emphasis will increasingly shift away from market selection toward stock selection, in our view, as a result of the much greater impact that global investors will have on equity markets worldwide. They will be shifting assets more and more between markets, and between similar stocks in different markets as a result of global research, ironing out some of the inefficiencies and making it increasingly difficult to time those markets. We're talking here about the impact, not just of the global investor coming out of the United States, but also the impact of the enormous increase in international investment from the United Kingdom in the last five years since exchange controls were lifted. We're seeing too, the Middle Eastern countries and the OPEC countries buying equities in quite large size now for the first time. Also, we're seeing the Japanese invest in international securities. So, I have a great deal of sympathy with what Bill Marshall indicated earlier, that value added is increasingly going to come from stock selection and less from market timing success. The broad-based decisions will cease to be the decisions on countries; rather, industry selection across countries will become the key macrodecision.

The Role of Currencies

So where does currency fit into the equation? In our experience, currency fluctuations have a relatively minor impact on investment returns. They have been far outweighed by the impact of being in the right markets and the right stocks. During 1983, for example, there was a great deal of money to be made in international investing despite the extreme strength of the dollar. But, it was made by being in the right markets and the right stocks. We think that reliance on a decision-making process driven by currency factors will hurt your overall strategy. It would have kept you out of the United Kingdom during the past few years, for example, which was a period of consistent underlying strength in the equity market. Currency factors, therefore, act to *moderate* our investment policy decisions rather than being a driving force behind them.

There are two principal caveats concerning this judgement. First, many investors still move for currency reasons—move into the Japanese equity market when they see a period of strength in the yen coming up, or move into the German or Swiss markets if they see strength in the DM or the Swiss franc, for example. So, we must watch the currencies, not only for their impact on returns (which can be significant in the short run) but also for their impact on how other investors perceive market opportunities.

The second caveat is that exchange rate factors can have a major impact on stock selection. During the past two years in Sweden, for example, it has been the international companies that have led the market as the weakness of the Krona comes straight through to the bottom line of companies like Asea, Ericsson, Astra and so forth. To have a specific example of the effect, consider that in the fourth quarter of 1982, the Swedish krona was devalued by 16 percent. The prices of Scandinavian multinationals instantly moved up 15–20 percent, making good the loss to the foreign investor.

THE U.K. MARKET

Against this background, I'd like now to talk more specifically about investing in the United Kingdom and in Scandinavia, beginning with the observation that the U.K. equity market is the third largest market in the world. At $200 billion in value, with over 2,500 companies listed and with about 25,000 transactions taking place daily, it serves the most sophisticated institutional investor base outside of the United States. It's a very active primary market, with a great deal of new issue and fund-raising activity. It is an extremely broadly-based market with 36 major industrial sectors and, of course, it's been one of the top performing markets in the world despite a generally lackluster economic background.

Recent Performance Criteria

There are two very clear reasons for that kind of performance, structural reasons inherent in the United Kingdom. The first is that there is an underrepresentation in the U.K. market of the slower-growth sectors such as utilities and basic industries. The reason, of course, is that they are state owned. Higher-growth sectors are, conversely, overrepresented. This gives the market an explosive quality and is one reason for the relative disparity between the performance of the U.K. market and that of the U.K. economy. The other key to that differential is that the U.K. market is a very international market, and over 50 percent of the earnings of U.K.-quoted companies are derived from exports or overseas services. Many U.K. international companies are, in effect, insulated from the slow growth of the domestic economy.

In broad terms, there are two distinct categories of stocks in the United Kingdom. One is comprised of the high-quality, high-growth, technology based and service industries. This category would include electricals, pharmaceuticals, financials, and retailers. These are the growth areas of the economy. They, on a long-term basis, should represent the heart of a U.K. portfolio because they are the driving force behind the economy and the equity market, constituting about 40 percent of total market value.

The second major area is the energy sector, which has grown up on the back of the North Sea development. It's the most important quoted energy sector outside the United States, and includes two of the "Seven Sisters" in BP and Shell. It's a very large sector and accounts for about 12 percent of total market value.

The remaining part of the market—about 45 percent—is concentrated in broad-range manufacturing sectors. These are typical "smokestack" companies, which remain highly cyclical, but they are far more efficient now than they were three years ago as a result of major rationalization measures completed in the very recent past. Over the past year, this group has led the market and has been an area of major cyclical recovery.

When the Oil Runs Out

I think it might be useful to say a few words on what happens when the oil runs out, because this is really something that long-term investors have to focus on. Production will peak in 1986 and will decline gradually—not rapidly—thereafter to a much lower base level. What does this mean for the United Kingdom, and what does it mean for stock selection? First, we've seen a massive restructuring of British industry, that has vastly increased its productivity. This was brought on primarily by the rise in Sterling during the period 1977–1980, a rise that was itself a function of North Sea oil revenues. Industry realized that it could no longer rely on constant devalua-

tions of the currency to boost its competitive position. The result was a series of more or less radical measures, now largely completed, to come to grips with that realization.

The second factor which should be taken into account regarding the oil question is something that the government undertook in 1979. That was the abolition of exchange controls, again made possible by the strength of Sterling as a result of North Sea oil flows. This has produced an enormous amount of direct and portfolio investment overseas in the ensuing four years. Britain has made use of the breathing space created by its oil revenues to rebuild its pre-war position, whereby last year the United Kingdom had a greater flow of income from overseas, from foreign assets, than in any year since 1945. This year, overseas investment income flowing into the United Kingdom will be about $13 billion, more than three times the level of 1978. So, oil has been the catalyst for a restructuring of the British industrial situation and for the creation of an overseas asset base. These will underpin the economy as North Sea production begins to fall away. This is mainly why we are comfortable on the long-term equation as far as oil is concerned.

Major Budget Considerations

Another important development is that we had a major financial statement from the government a short while ago, in the form of an annual budget statement that is going to have very significant long-term effects on the U.K. economy. It is going to reverse the market performance of the past year or so (i.e., the overperformance of the cyclical sectors). This is because a key item in the budget is a reduction of the U.K. corporation tax over three years, from 52 percent to 35 percent, while tax allowances are simultaneously phased out. Why should this be so significant and have such profound implications for sector performance over time?

First of all, the enormous range of domestic tax rates paid by different companies will disappear. Second, for each company, tax rates will become much more stable rather than fluctuating wildly from year to year. Third, intercompany comparisons will become much more valid and, most importantly, U.K. analysis will reflect earnings on the basis of the actual tax paid rather than on the basis of full notional rates. This is common practice in the United States, but it is not now the case in the United Kingdom. It's one of the reasons why ICI, for example, might appear cheap to U.S. investors but fully valued to U.K. investors. In the future, the domestic investors who still dominate the U.K. market will calculate P/E ratios on the basis of actual tax paid at 35 percent rather than on a notional rate of 52%. As a result, the P/E multiple of the market drops from 14 to around 11. It's quite interesting to note that the new rate of 35 percent set by the Chancellor was exactly the level of the average tax rate in the United Kingdom last year.

It is the growth sectors of the economy that are going to benefit from this change—the insurance brokers, the retailers, and so forth, who have been paying taxes at around the full 52 percent rate because they couldn't take advantage of capital allowances. Conversely, tax rates may rise in the manufacturing sectors, where tax payments have been much lower because of major capital allowances. The government's objective is absolutely clear: It wants to encourage the growth sectors in the economy. They see those sectors as being the future driving force behind the economy, and they see those sectors as being the key to getting unemployment down.

The government is also beginning to tackle the institutional domination of the market. Over 60 percent of the market is owned by institutions who carry out over 70 percent of all trading. As well, the government is beginning to tackle the tax incentives that have operated in favor of institutions and against the individual. The net effect is to encourage saving and investment in the United Kingdom and even to encourage the identification, for example, of the individual's prosperity with that of his or her company through a much wider incidence of share ownership. The government has clearly decided to move toward the encouragement of a share-owning democracy as well as a house-owning democracy. These are important decisions that should have favorable long term effects on the attraction of the U.K. markets to global investors.

THE SCANDANAVIAN MARKETS

To complete my presentation I will comment rather more briefly on Scandinavia, which is in some ways almost a unique investment area. It is tiny, irrelevant in index terms at less than 1.5 percent of the Capital International World Index.

Yet, you have in Scandinavia an extraordinary concentration of well managed, technologically strong, and very advanced high-growth companies. Most of them are household names to international investors and many of them are very familiar to U.S. investors.

High-Quality, High-Growth Companies Available

The index weightings are in no way representative of the importance of the underlying companies. The Danish company Novo constitutes 25 percent of the Danish index. Over 60 percent of the Norwegian index is concentrated in just two sectors: energy and data processing. And 40 percent of the Swedish index is also in only two sectors: electricals and electronics, and health care. We believe that many of the companies involved are sufficiently high-quality and high-growth to represent long-term, core holdings in globally-diversified portfolios. The question we ask ourselves is not whether they should be included, but simply when. Most of these companies have a very limited dependence on their home markets, with the average being maybe 80 percent of sales from overseas. When we look at Scandinavia we look at the markets purely on a stock-by-stock basis, and the fact that the companies are Scandinavian is almost incidental. In particular, we are looking to take advantage of the valuation anomalies that produce such opportunities as being able, three years ago, to buy Ericsson at four times earnings despite its technological base in telecommunications, while Nippon Electric, with maybe an equal technological position, was selling at 40 times earnings. Today, you can buy Asea, a Swedish company with about an equal worldwide market share in robotics as Fanuc of Japan, at less than seven times earnings versus maybe 50 times for Fanuc. That seems like a valuation anomaly to us.

Local Economics Relatively Unimportant

We're not particularly concerned with the growth rates of the country economies in Scandinavia, or even with political developments, which at present don't exert much influence on the market. If there is a macro overlay for our stock selection approach to Scandinavia it is confined to an analysis of the supply and demand for funds (i.e., to an analysis of the technical background of the market). To some extent, Scandinavia is a cash flow game and the recent arrival of the foreign investor has accentuated this. In addition, in all three countries there are significant tax incentives in place to encourage domestic investment in the equity markets.

To sum up on Scandinavia, the background to the market strength of the past two to three years has been due to three factors. First, a very strong underlying trading performance from the high growth, high quality companies. Second, a 55 percent fall in the value of the Swedish krona against the dollar. And last, a very favorable technical background in the market. The position today is that the underlying growth in many of those companies is still good. They're not going to grow as fast because they're much bigger than they were two or three years ago, but they will continue to grow at attractive rates without any further kick from the currency.

FUTURE SHARE PRICES KEYED TO GLOBAL FACTORS

A trend has begun that will continue throughout the 1980s whereby companies trading internationally are being evaluated not on local criteria but on global criteria, against their worldwide competition. Thus, two-tier markets are becoming increasingly common. In this environment, the share prices of international companies will become less and less correlated with domestic share prices and more and more subject to international investor perceptions and valuation criteria.

Global Investment Portfolios: Continental Europe

Ivan Pictet

To me, international investing is a constant series of trade-offs. Global portfolio management entails balancing macroissues of currency and country weightings against microissues of industry emphasis and stock selection. I favor a top-down approach, with four main elements: country selection, currency selection, industry selection, and stock selection. Of these, the elements of currency and country selection rank first in importance.

CONTINENTAL EUROPEAN OVERVIEW

Not a Single Investment Region

As an investment alternative to the United States, the Far East, or the United Kingdom, Continental Europe cannot be considered as one single investment region. Rather, it comprises a diverse group of countries with a total population of 290 million and a combined GNP of $1,750 billion. As shown in Figure 1, it is a major component of the western world's economic activity, but it is very different

from other investment or economic regions owing to its diversity. Continental Europe includes 13 different countries offering many investment opportunities, with as many currencies, legal and regulatory environments, and almost as many languages. Furthermore, the size of its equity markets is proportionately much smaller than for other regions, with a total capitalization of about $280 billion. This is due to a variety of factors, in particular to the size of the nationalized sector in France, which has reduced its market capitalization substantially, and the tendency for German companies not to go public before they are very mature. As a result of this diversity, domestic influences on European markets are often more significant than the worldwide trend dictated by Wall Street. Economic policies, local political developments, and market psychology represent major factors influencing European capital markets.

Figure 2 shows how the different major country markets have progressed since the beginning of 1982. It is obvious that not all the money in this bull market has been made in the United

FIGURE 1
European aggregate characteristics relative to the free world

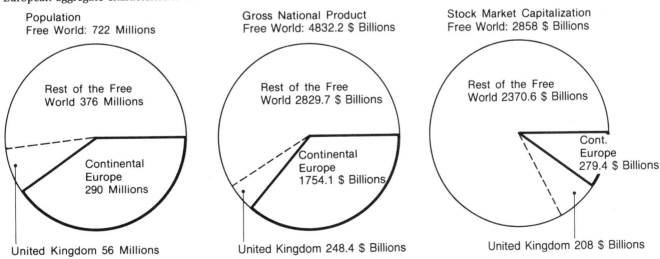

Population
Free World: 722 Millions

Rest of the Free World 376 Millions

Continental Europe 290 Millions

United Kingdom 56 Millions

Gross National Product
Free World: 4832.2 $ Billions

Rest of the Free World 2829.7 $ Billions

Continental Europe 1754.1 $ Billions

United Kingdom 248.4 $ Billions

Stock Market Capitalization
Free World: 2858 $ Billions

Rest of the Free World 2370.6 $ Billions

Cont. Europe 279.4 $ Billions

United Kingdom 208 $ Billions

FIGURE 2
Selection of stock market indexes in local currencies

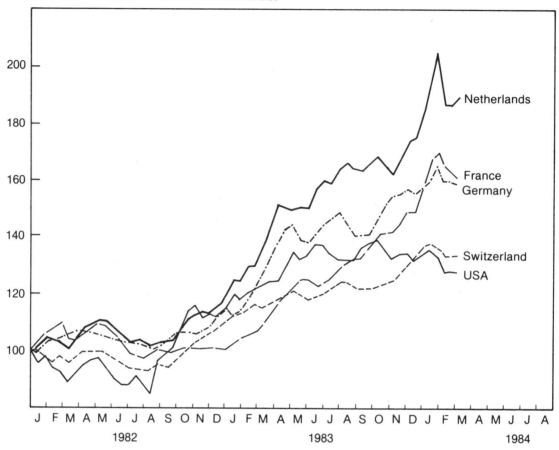

States Even in this rather exceptional period of general market euphoria, you will notice significant differences in country performance.

Emphasis on National Factors

To tackle the diversity of Continental Europe for investment, Pictet & Cie use mostly a top-down approach which leads to the identification and evaluation of national factors. Once the allocation decision is complete, stock research may reveal situations justifying a change in that allocation. Typically, attractive stocks in smaller markets may lead to larger commitments to those markets than was indicated by the asset allocation process.

Our top-down approach focuses on the following decision elements:

A/B—Currency and country selection, on the same level of importance;

C—Industry selection; and
D—Stock selection.

Country and currency selection are put on the same level for the following reasons:

- In practice, most portfolios bear the country risk and the currency risk simultaneously and very few investors use systematic currency hedges to separate the currency decision from the country decision.
- A country with a weak currency can have a very strong equity market, and vice versa.

Considering the four elements in detail:

TOP-DOWN APPROACH EXAMPLE

Currency Selection Factors

Currency forecasting is probably the area that has caused the most frustration to economic forecasters and investment strategists. The main fundamental variables that determine exchange rates are:

- Purchasing power parity
- Current account (trade balance)
- Interest rates

The problem arises from the fact that these variables influence exchange rates over the long run only. Shorter term, relying exclusively on these variables leads to miserable results because money market expectations and market psychology are such powerful factors.

Illustrating the purchasing power parity aspect, Figure 3 shows the effective nominal and real exchange rates of the United States, the United Kingdom, and Switzerland over the last 10 years (real rates are trade-weighted exchange rates). It is, of course, difficult to determine the correct value of a currency on a purchasing power basis, but it is a fact that even when a currency seems overvalued, it can become significantly more so or remain overvalued for a long period of time before returning to equilibrium, and vice versa.

Figure 4 shows that a similar problem exists with respect to current (trade) accounts. Although a country cannot run current account deficits without effect forever, it can run them without affecting its exchange rate as long as it can easily attract capital to finance its current deficit. Over the last three years, the U.S. current deficit has grown steadily, without preventing the dollar from appreciating, for example. The lack of fore-

FIGURE 3
Purchasing power parity effective

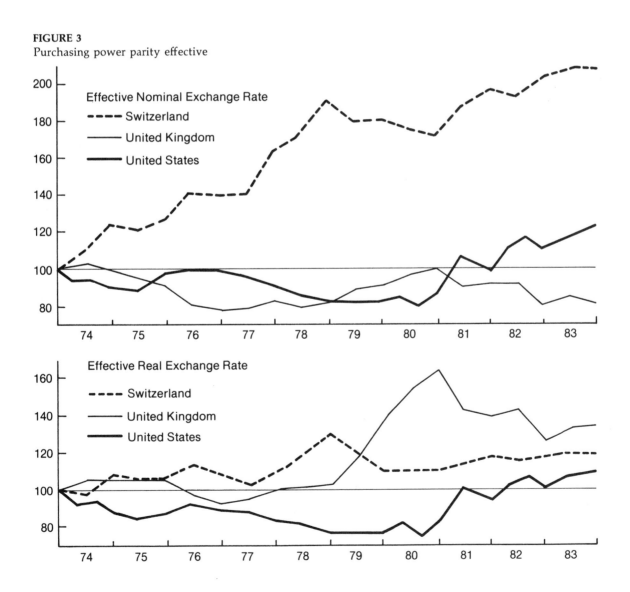

FIGURE 4
Current account and effective nominal exchange rate

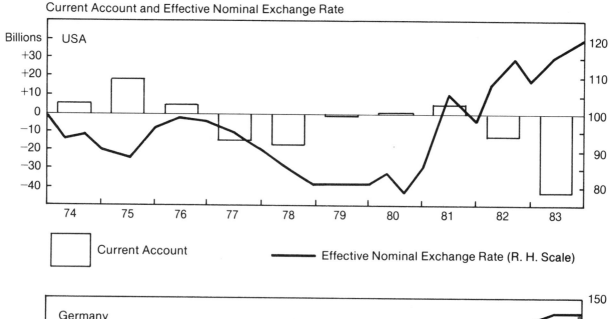

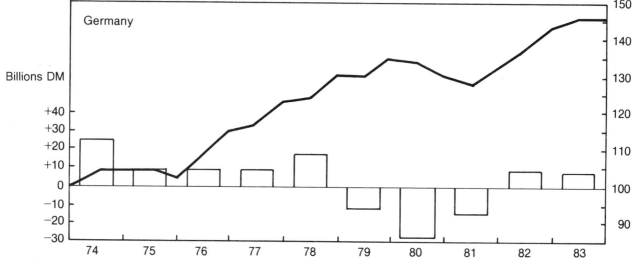

casting power of fundamental variables can partly be associated with the emergence of vast flows of funds that are totally free to move quickly and massively from one country to another. They can easily offset the flows generated by the local economy.

Within Europe, fortunately, an area of relative stability has been created by means of the European Monetary System (EMS). Although the EMS has not eliminated currency fluctuations, it has significantly reduced their volatility. Survival of the EMS in the face of widely divergent economic policies (particularly between France and Germany) has necessitated frequent readjust-

ment of rates within the EMS. The name of the game then is to forecast EMS realignments.

These are sometimes easy to forecast but difficult to take advantage of, because differences in short-term rates most often incorporate an implied realignment that is also translated into the forward exchange rates. For example, the French raised short-term French franc rates as much as necessary last year in order to deter speculators and postpone a realignment until after the municipal elections. Figure 5 shows the French franc–DM relationship before and after this event. Not all realignments are anticipated, however, and "surprise" realignments are always possible.

FIGURE 5
March 83 European Monetary System realignment

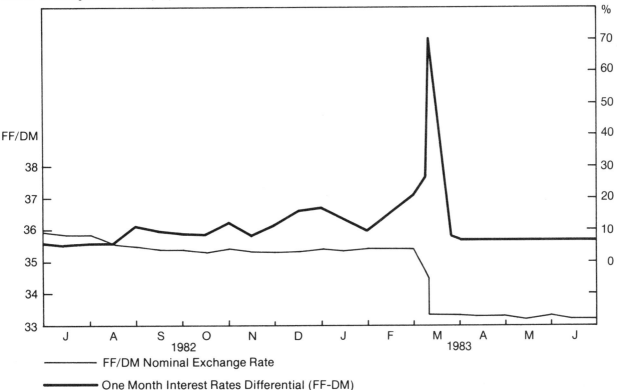

——————— FF/DM Nominal Exchange Rate

━━━━━ One Month Interest Rates Differential (FF-DM)

These tend to be more effective because they prevent speculation rather than merely respond to it.

In summary, exchange rates are determined in the short-term by market expectations and market psychology. As such, the currency is an asset just like bonds and shares. Over the longer run (which is not very relevant for portfolio managers), fundamental political trends are the key to the determination of exchange rates. In the last thirty years, for instance, the Germans have always given top priority to defense of the currency, while the French always seem to find more important political priorities. Figure 6 illustrates the FF-DM currency effect of these very different emphases.

Country Selection Factors

Country selection is a key decision parameter in Europe because several key variables affecting the level of the stock market are essentially national:

- Political changes;
- Monetary/fiscal policy orientation;

- Supply and demand factors on capital markets (institutional cash-flow/foreign investors' involvment); and
- Legal, tax and regulatory environments (e.g. tax incentives for equity investors, and so on).

These national factors fully justify a top-down approach, in our view.

Common external factors are obviously also very important, for instance, the worldwide business cycle and the influence of monetary policy abroad. However, these factors are more important for global market timing decisions than for the identification of countries likely to outperform the averages. Therefore, country selection is based first on a set of fundamental variables that affect stock market performance over the medium term.

- Economic growth (Table 1 illustrates the current forecast);
- Corporate profit growth (Table 1 illustrates the current forecast);

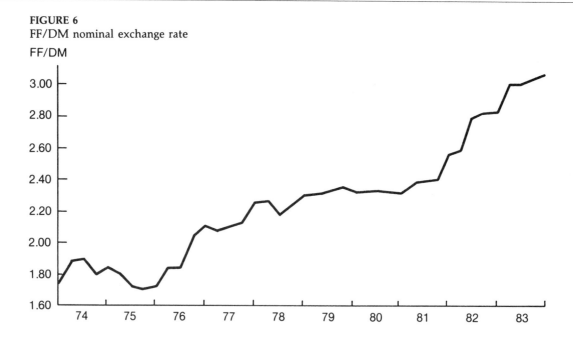

FIGURE 6
FF/DM nominal exchange rate

FF/DM

- Valuation (earnings yield and yield growth relative to long-term government yields); and
- Politics.

Changes in these variables and in expectations are the key to portfolio decisions. This is where the international observer has an advantage over the domestic investor—local participants are often myopic with respect to worldwide developments affecting their own country's growth and competitiveness.

Another significant aspect in country selection is the market's relative liquidity and supply/demand situation. In connection with these, the following questions need to be answered:

- Is there an important private pension fund system? If so, what is its cash flow?
- Are there particular incentives to promote equity ownership (as, for example, in France, Belgium, Sweden, and Norway)?

- What is the current level of mutual fund sales and what are their cash positions relative to historical levels?
- Are foreign investors already in this market?

This last factor, the role of foreign investors, has become increasingly important in the last few years. With the internationalization of U.S. institutions, and the "rediscovery" of Continental Europe by U.K. fund managers, increasingly large pools of funds move freely from market to market. As they are free from institutional constraints, they can move *out* of a country completely, or move *in* aggressively when the situation changes. In small markets, this can lead to major market distortions. Therefore, one of the problems (and opportunities) in selecting countries in Europe is to determine what one's competitors are up to.

Criteria for Industry Selection

The first question here is whether a global European industry approach is appropriate. It does not appear to us to be so. A single industry can be subject to divergent influences in different countries. Retail can be interesting in Switzerland but not in France. A German engineering firm can suffer from the same factor that makes its Swedish competitors attractive, namely a Swedish devaluation.

TABLE 1.   Real GNP and corporate profit growth

	Real GNP growth		Corporate profit growth
	1980–1983	*1984E*	*1984E*
West Germany	+0.4%	+2.5%	+18%
France	+0.8	+1.0	+20
Switzerland	+1.4	+2.0	+10
Netherlands	−0.3	+1.0	+20
Sweden	+0.9	+2.2	+20

Currencies play a major role; in weak currency countries, exporters are prosperous while importers' margins are squeezed and retailers usually suffer. Take the example of Sweden and its forest product industry, which benefited for a number of years until 1983 from several devaluations. After the Socialist victory in France and the EMS realignment, retailers were hurt, exporters of consumer goods did extremely well, and multinationals suffered from large currency losses on their foreign debt.

Within a single country, however, an industry approach is absolutely necessary. Macroeconomic developments, domestic and international, have a large impact. The international investor has an advantage over the local participant as he will see changes more rapidly through the cross-fertilization of investment ideas. Also, the international investor can make a specific industry bet in any country while the domestic investor will tend to spread his holdings generally over the whole market.

Criteria for Stock Selection

This topic has been covered at length by other seminar participants. I will simply note that, because accounting practices, disclosure rules, and so on vary greatly from country to country and often between companies, quality research is a tremendous source of added value.

In addition, the internationalization of the investment scene is a new and important factor in stock selection. Increasingly, international in-

TABLE 2. Pictet country allocation matrix February 1984		
	Capital International Index capitalization weighting	Pictet & Cie allocation
North America	56.4%	38%
Far East	23.0	19
United Kingdom	8.0	6
West Germany	3.2	8
France	1.4	1
Switzerland	1.7	7
Netherlands	1.6	3
Belgium	0.4	3
Sweden	0.9	1
Italy	0.9	1
Others	2.5%	—
Cash and equivalent	—	13

vestors are comparing companies across national borders. This can result in the revaluation of multiples when a crowd of international investors steps in (as, for example, in the case of Philips, Royal Dutch, and Daimler-Benz). As a result, there is a new game in Europe: identifying likely candidates for a New York listing, with a hoped-for revaluation of the stock.

As shown in Table 2, our own firm's current allocation to the seven major countries is 24 percent versus a CIEAFE Index weighting of about 10 percent for the same group. The area is in a very attractive phase right now. If you feel a bit confused after this presentation, I will have succeeded in conveying the great diversity of Continental Europe.

Global Investment Portfolios: Japan

Robert J. Boyd

I will talk a little about investment philosophy particularly as it applies to Japan.

As a general observation, if there were a "perfect investment" it might be considered as one from which returns would increase faster, for longer, and with a greater degree of consistency than was generally expected. Thus, it could be bought at a valuation level which did not reflect those prospects. Conversely, the "worst investment" would be one whose present price reflected great hopes for the future, which were immediately disappointed.

LOOKING AT JAPAN FOR INVESTMENT

A Maturing Economy

For over twenty years Japan's gross national product grew at a 10 percent per annum rate in real terms, fueled by extraordinarily high rates of savings and capital expenditure by the private sector. About 10 years ago, the rate of growth began to slow, mainly because the "easy" ways of growing had by then been largely exploited. The big shift of labor out of inefficient agriculture into highly productive industry had taken place, and industry itself, having caught up with the products and processes of the West, had found that there were fewer opportunities to copy and learn from other industrialized countries. The only way forward was the more difficult and expensive route of research and innovation. In other words, the Japanese economy was maturing.

The process of maturing has been gradual, and even in the late 1970s the Japanese economy was still capable of growing at more than five percent per annum. The hard work, thoroughness, high productivity, and propensity to save which stood the Japanese in good stead in the relatively easy "catch-up" years are also important qualities when growth is led by research and innovation. Now, the torrent of personal savings is more likely to finance research laboratories or factory reorganizations rather than green-field development, but with no less urgency. Nonethe-

less, growth is undeniably harder to achieve and, in the past three years, the average growth rate has been nearer to three percent than to five percent.

It is therefore ironic that foreigners' enthusiasm for investment in Japan has grown enormously only in the past few years, just when the overall rate of economic growth has been slowing down. Furthermore, the prices that foreigners have had to pay for Japanese equities have risen enormously, even though corporate profit growth has also slowed in line with the economy. In 1974, the average P/E of the market was about 15 times. Today, it is over 25 times. As recently as 1980, Hitachi—a company representative of the economy as a whole—was trading at six times earnings. Today, it stands at 15 times. Similar re-ratings have occurred for numerous other major, good quality companies. If people take into account differences in accounting practices and taxation, the Japanese stock market appears to be more highly rated (priced) than any other major stock market. Why should this be so?

Factors Influencing Valuation Levels

A number of reasons suggest themselves. There is a possibility that investors are prepared to pay up in the expectation not only of growth, but also of stability and predictability. The re-rating of the Japanese stock market over the past 10 years has occurred in line with a progressive re-orientation of economic policy in Japan. In contrast to the boom and bust cycles of economic activity and cyclically rising levels of inflation which characterized the 1960s and the 1970s, the Japanese economy has been noted for stable prices, stable interest rates, and steady, albeit lower, economic growth rates.

Some elements of this stability were in place a lot earlier—political stability, for instance. The same center-right, pro-business party has been in power since the 1950s. While Prime Ministers have come and gone, government fiscal policy continues to be determined by the powerful bureaucrats of the Ministry of Finance. The basic tax schedules, depreciation allowances, and principles of taxation have been unaltered for years. The system remains blessedly uncluttered with special concessions for tax "incentives." Equitable or not, the tax system does not spring surprises on the private sector and the rules of the game are not rewritten each year at budget time.

In the West, much is made of the supposed collaboration between Japanese industry and government; in fact, the government's financial support is token (by the standards of most countries). The public sector as a whole takes only a small slice of the economy. As a result, taxes are not only stable, but also low.

Financial Stability—A Key Consideration

From an investment point of view, what we consider to be of equal or greater importance has been the impressive stability of monetary policy. Since 1974, the Bank of Japan has taken control of the money supply as its main objective. The central bank has not only set progressively lower and lower targets for monetary growth, it has also consistently met those targets. In a perfect demonstration of the textbook monetarism of Milton Friedman, the Bank of Japan has brought inflation down from over 25 percent per annum 10 years ago to negligible levels in recent years. Wholesale prices have been flat for four years, consumer price inflation is under two percent and the broadest measure of inflation, the GNP deflator, is actually negative. In such an environment, interest rates are low and stable, and inflation expectations have melted away.

The steady monetary policy has also smoothed out the business cycle, just as Friedman predicted it would. In good years the economy grows by 5 percent; in bad years, 3 percent. Monetary policy has not been used to stimulate demand. The biggest sources of instability have instead been external, as the oil shocks, for examples, and cyclical surges and declines in overseas demands for Japanese exports.

The Japanese economy is not growing faster than its sustainable rate, the currency is undervalued and the consensus belief is that if interest rates move at all, the next move will be down, not up. Although liquidity will eventually tighten in Japan as domestic demand, inventory building, and capital expenditure take up the slack, there is little reason to expect it to tighten either soon or suddenly. The biggest macroeconomic risk is probably in the dollar, which is living on bor-

rowed time and borrowed money. As it falls, the rate of growth of U.S. imports will eventually slow down to grow no faster, and probably more slowly, than the U.S. GNP for a time. When that happens, the rate of growth and stability of Japanese exports, especially of more traditional goods, will deteriorate. For the economy as a whole, however, and therefore for the majority of companies, the outlook would appear both favorable and stable. Current valuation levels indicate that participants share this outlook with a high degree of confidence.

Financing the Technology Factor

How justifiable is this confidence? Apart from expectations concerning the overall economic and financial environment, and especially the expectation of future stability, confidence seems largely to be based on the belief that Japan has a growing advantage in exploiting the opportunities of the technological revolution. The momentum behind the advance of Japanese companies into strategic new industries is hard to overestimate. By and large, huge commitments of capital to the new technologies have been effectively and profitably invested.

One of the origins of this success is the well-known propensity of Japanese companies to plan further ahead than some of their competitors in other countries, and to be more diligent and painstaking about quality and reliability. It is not surprising that the world, within Japan and without, is rushing to finance Japanese industry through high-priced equity and low-coupon debt.

An important advantage also comes from the Japanese financial system itself: Japanese companies have access to extraordinarily cheap capital. Social conventions mean that unfriendly takeovers are virtually unheard of. Furthermore, shareholders have little effective influence on the management of companies. Since ownership does not imply control, companies have few qualms about diluting their shareholders. Equity finance is regarded as little more than another source of funds. Many American companies must envy Nippon Electric, which can get away with paying a dividend that yields 0.5 percent and can raise money in the stock market at 5 times book value. Recently, Japanese companies have been issuing Swiss Franc convertible bonds with coupons as low as 1-3/4 percent, at conversion premiums of 10 percent to the price of the common stock and with minimal underwriting fees.

Aggressive companies have used cheap equity financing with formidable effects. Murata Seisakusho, a manufacturer of electronic components, has more than tripled its manufacturing plant in the past three years—in the midst of a very severe worldwide recession and while it was experiencing weak demand for its products. This expansion was financed mainly by shareholders, yet because the stock was highly rated the extra plant generated more than enough profits to offset the dilution. Sales doubled, profits rose 150 percent, and earnings per share grew 70 percent. Not a bad return in just three years. To take another example, the leading Japanese machine tool companies have been raising capital in the stock market at four times book value and at P/E multiples around 40 times peak earnings. A very good, if unpublicized, reason for the American and the West German machine tool industries to be worried about Japanese competition.

The Japanese are nothing if not opportunistic, and with so many obliging investors so ready to provide so much money so cheaply, it is not surprising that Japanese companies should exploit the situation while it lasts. For the investor, however, what are the prospects of earning his expected return? The last railway to be built in Britain never made a profit. Neither did the later, more esoteric "alternative energy" projects in the United States. The grander office blocks now being completed in Hong Kong are a headache to the owners, not to mention their financiers. Each of these investment mistakes rose from the classic boom and bust cycle in which investors fell over themselves to put money into the fad of the moment. What makes the "High Tech" boom different, perhaps, is that the money is chasing a moving target.

Why Japanese "High Tech" May Be for Real

As an example, just when it was felt that the world was being oversupplied with 16K chips, the battleground shifted to the 64k, which spawned a whole new range of products and profitable opportunities. The 256K chip is now poised to carry the baton. And each time, the Japanese gained a greater share of the world market. Unlike the demand for oil, or for property in Hong Kong, there is no theoretical limit to demand for something as intangible as information processing. It is not easy to estimate the potential demand for each successive generation of integrated circuits, or how the widespread, instant, and cheap transmission of data will transform society. The greatest profits are to be found where the fastest rate of change is taking place, and there is no sign that the pace of change in electronics technology is slackening.

For these very reasons, however, it is tremendously important to back the winners. As the number of contestants increases, so do the risks and uncertainties. Last year, several hundred new companies came to the market in the United States, many of them in the technology sector. By contrast, most Japanese companies sporting "High Tech" labels are fundamentally of a different character. They are for the most part, subsidiaries or affiliates of immensely powerful zaibatsu groups. They are backed by banks and brokers and have access to the research laboratories and even to the personnel of their parents. They enjoy substantial intergroup markets, and the giants are not going to crush them because they are authorized suppliers to the giants. They are also relatively scarce: Last year, in all, only two dozen new companies came to the market. Providing an investor is diligent in assessing the friends and connections of the company, and can see it developing a strategic market position in its field, then the fundamental risk in such an investment is much less than its mere size would suggest.

However, if the portfolio manager does not have to "Bank of Japan-Watch" in Japan the way he must "Fed-Watch" in the United States, it is equally insufficient for him to confine his analytical endeavors to judging the potential in the marketplace for products and services, or to swings in supply and demand. There are a number of pitfalls for the unwary foreign investment manager which give investment in Japan a unique flavor.

UNIQUE MARKET CONSIDERATIONS IMPORTANT

One of the most striking facts of life in the Japanese market is the power of the brokers. The market is only a third of the size of the U.S. market, but it is the stamping ground for a brokerage house which last year earned more than Merrill Lynch on its revenues of $1.6 billion. This giant, Nomura Securities, has a 16 percent market share, bigger than ML's 12 percent share in New York or Hoare Govett's 7 percent share in London. Moreover, Nomura is just the largest of a group of heavyweights—known as the Big Four—who, with their satellites, have 75 percent of the market under their control. These statistics tell only part of the story. Not only are the brokers strong, but their clients are weak.

Volume Still Dominated by Individuals

Domestic institutional investors still account for less than a quarter of trading, compared to 75 percent in the United States. A large proportion of this is directly and indirectly controlled by the Big Four anyway. Meanwhile, private individual investors, who account for nearly 60 percent of the trading, can be corralled by aggressive salesmen into a particular "Stock of the Week." With so much influence on so much money, a recommendation by one of these brokers has the ability to move even very large stocks in a gravity-defying manner. Whether a broker is just beginning or is in the course of a major selling campaign can be very important for investment timing. Sale recommendations need not, however, be feared, although the absence of attention following a major promotion can lead to lackluster performance for many months, or even years.

For the most part, the individual investor pays little attention to conventional security analysis. Anyhow, the retail salesman would not normally supply him with anything so distracting as facts and figures. The technical vocabulary of the Japanese market is thus filled with terms like "Lantern Buying," "Dream Stocks," "Incentive-Backed Issues," "Charm Points," and "Blue Sky." Concepts play an important role in determining whether a given stock becomes a high flier.

Role of Foreign Investors

Although a relatively small number of overseas institutions, often specialists, have been active and significant investors in Japan for over two decades, it is only in the past few years that foreign investors in general have stepped into this exotic and emotional world on a really substantial scale. Five years ago foreign institutions owned two percent of the Japanese market; now they own seven percent. They now account for 20 percent of the trading, which is almost as much as

done by domestic Japanese institutions. By and large, these foreigners brought with them the analytical methods that they grew up with in their own markets. Traditionally, they found the Japanese market riddled with anomalies. They found fast-growing, excellent companies at multiple levels less than half of the market as a whole. Sometimes a company would look expensive in the conventional Japanese-style accounts, but be revealed to look extraordinarily cheap when properly consolidated income statements were prepared. The flood of foreign money into such stocks created an impressive bull market in quality issues in the past three years, and for most of this period foreign portfolio managers found it relatively easy to outperform the stock market indexes by a substantial amount. In fact, the success of the foreign investor has been so striking that perceptive domestic Japanese investors have taken to tracking and copying the foreign investors' moves. In many cases what started as a foreign investor's modest accumulation of shares on weak days has been overtaken by frantic buying from domestic speculators. Many foreigners now shake their heads in amazement at the heights to which their favorite shares have risen.

A cluster of high technology issues now stand at P/E multiples well up in the 80s and even in the hundreds. At the same time, the compliment has been returned by some of the foreigners who, seeing that price movements and valuation levels did not necessarily conform to what they were accustomed to at home, have adopted a more "Japanese" approach for investment decision making. Research reports from Tokyo are full of terms such as "export-related" or "office automation-related." Foreigners sometimes use the more succinct expression "going up-related."

Share-Supply and Liquidity
Considerations

Another factor that has contributed to elevating stock prices in recent years, particularly for small companies, is the shortage of supply. Until last year the requirements a company had to satisfy in order to obtain a stock market listing were very stringent. By the time that companies had grown large enough and profitable enough to satisfy the requirements, they were already well into middle age. Even though the Japanese market is capitalized at nearly $600 billion—over a third of the capitalization of the U.S. market—the number of listed companies is only 1,800 compared to over 8,000 issues in the United States. Over the past ten years the Tokyo Stock Exchange Index has doubled, and total market capitalization has gone up three and one-half times, but the number of listed companies has increased by only seven percent. Over the past five years, over 1,600 companies were floated in the U.S. market, compared with a mere 68 in Japan. As one might expect, because of the relative scarcity of fast-growing small companies, they command a huge market premium.

An additional factor restricting the supply of stock and tending to cause volatile price movements is the large amount of stock in firm hands. It is estimated that 65 percent of the stock market is owned for political or strategic purposes by companies and banks who hold shares not primarily for investment but to cement business relationships. Such holdings are rarely traded. A representative example of this phenomena is Ando Electric, a company with annual sales of $120 million and a strong position in textile equipment and optical fiber communications equipment. Fundamentally a highly attractive issue, over half of its shares are locked away in the hands of Nippon Electric and other companies in the Sumitomo Group. Foreign institutional investors now own four million shares, leaving two million for domestic investors. The daily trading volume is zero for days on end and the price has been driven to a P/E of 80 in the current bull market. In a bear market, these favorable dynamics can go all too quickly into reverse. Fortunately, for the past 20 years, the Japanese market has been remarkably forgiving. The mistake foreign investors usually make is to underestimate the euphoria of the Japanese investment community, and therefore the upside potential of Japanese stocks.

LONG-TERM PERSPECTIVE ESSENTIAL

To conclude, how should the investment analyst look at Japan? I think there are three basic questions, and they're the same fundamental ones you must ask anywhere. Is Japan going to grow faster than other countries? Is it going to grow with a greater degree of predictability or consistency than other countries? Is it overvalued?

Underlying Dynamics Favor Future Growth

I think that in looking at Japan one should stand back and relax a little bit, and try not to take it too seriously. Remember that we're in a marathon, not a sprint. With the market up, we're susceptible to a defensive situation in which America is probably what to focus on. I think when we flip to change, Japan is an incredibly dynamic country. Although some things never change, there are other aspects that do change very, very rapidly and dramatically. Undiscounted change is a source of profit opportunity, and the analyst must be constantly alert to it. In Japan, as anywhere else, one must try to invest in strong management. That's hard to be sure of in a very different cultural and economic environment, but it is still important. The analyst must also strive to find earnings acceleration that has not yet been discounted; if he can do it in Japan, he can do it anywhere! I think that if you do those things, follow this kind of course, the results will be favorable. I tend to believe that searching for value in Japan, pursued as an end in itself, will prove more or less fruitless; but a pragmatic, diligent, highly professional, and equally opportunistic approach to research will actually produce value very effectively over time.

Global Investment Portfolios: The Resource Countries—Australia, Singapore, and Malaysia

Jeremy D. Paulson-Ellis

When one thinks of minerals and natural resources, one naturally thinks of Australia, Canada, and South Africa. I will concentrate, however, on Australia, Singapore, and Malaysia, the latter two perhaps being more aptly classified as "resource" countries than as "mineral" countries. While Malaysia produces about one-third of the world's tin output, it receives more income from its exports of rubber, palm oil, timber, and petroleum. Singapore has very little in the way of natural resources. However, it has historically been a re-export center for much of Malaysia's and Indonesia's commodities, and nearly 30 percent of its exports are petroleum-based products. The links between the stock markets in Singapore and Malaysia are close. Although there are separate stock exchanges in Singapore and Kuala Lumpur, over 80 percent of the approximately 285 listed stocks are quoted on both markets.

COUNTRY INVESTMENT BACKGROUNDS

In world market terms, these three countries are not large. The equity market capitalization at the end of 1983 for Australia was valued at only $56 billion U.S., while Singapore was at $45 billion and Malaysia was around $30 billion. These are obviously minuscule in comparison to domestic equities on the New York Stock Exchange valued at $1,500 billion. In volume terms, the markets show similar trends. In spite of their sizes, however, these markets continue to attract a high degree of attention from investors worldwide. This reflects the opportunity to achieve higher returns by investing in growth areas. In well-balanced portfolios, investments in the above countries should add significantly to the return without adding unduly to the portfolio's overall risk exposure. In practice, I believe that between 10 percent and 15 percent of an international portfolio may be in resource stocks, with some trading up and down between these two limits.

Experience in Australia

The potential from doing this and the out-performance of the markets at various times are illustrated in Figure 1, which shows the dollar-adjusted performance of the Australian market in relation to the U.S. market, as measured by the Standard & Poor's composite index (left-hand scale). It is immediately apparent that the Australian market is a more volatile one.

Although the graph shows that buying Australian stocks can lead to higher returns, one has to note that the correlation between the Australian market and the New York stock exchange is relatively high. Indeed, the London Business School has estimated the average correlation to be among the highest correlations existing between any two markets. This correlation has probably altered over the last two years, but will undoubtedly still be high. Australia, for U.S. investors, is a trading market.

One possible explanation for the high correlation of the two markets is the close relationship which exists between the relative performance and the rate of inflation in the U.S., which is measured on the right-hand scale. As United States inflation picks up, we believe that fund managers seek protection of the real value of their portfolios and move more into resource stocks. The higher each portfolio manager thinks U.S. inflation will go, the greater the outflow and the more, therefore, Australia has to offer. In fact, the impact of foreign portfolio investment on the Australian market is quite strong. This was particularly evident throughout the 1978–1981 period and, I suspect, is a factor in the latest rise.

The constituent parts of the rises are virtually all owing to the out-performance of the Australian market (see Table 1). The currency effect was also favorable. In two of the three periods in which a rise occurred, the currency gain alone provided a return exceeding the return on the Standard & Poor's index.

FIGURE 1
Australia/US currency-adjusted relative and US inflation

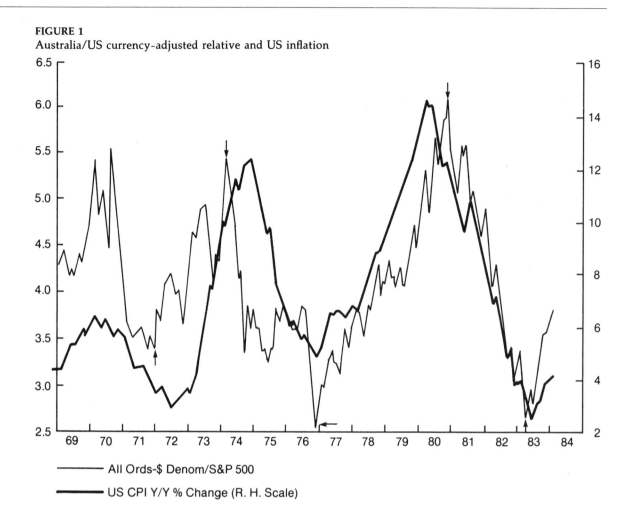

—— All Ords-$ Denom/S&P 500

—— US CPI Y/Y % Change (R. H. Scale)

Experience in Singapore and Malaysia

A similar cyclical pattern in the Singapore market is illustrated in Figure 2. In this case, however, a basic upward trend also exists. This trend disguises a cyclical pattern which, although not as well defined as in Australia, is still present. The left scale refers to the relative currency adjusted performance, while the right scale measures U.S. inflation. The upward trend seems to reflect the expanding industrialization of Singapore and the high growth achieved.

With Singapore's move into high-margin products, the upward trend should continue. The result is a relative decline of re-export activity in such items as crude rubber, timber, and coffee, all of which contribute strongly to the cyclical pattern. Even so, the resource aspect of this market is still sufficient to attract international investors.

TABLE 1.   Australian market

	11/71–4/74	12/76–11/80	8/83–2/84
Total relative change	68.4%	136.6%	57.9%
S&P Composite Index (U.S.)	−2.3	23.5	4.0
All Ordinaries Index (Austr.)	28.4	151.7	54.8
A$/US$	28.1	16.1	5.1
Duration of move (months)	29	47	11

FIGURE 2
Singapore/US currency-adjusted relative and US inflation

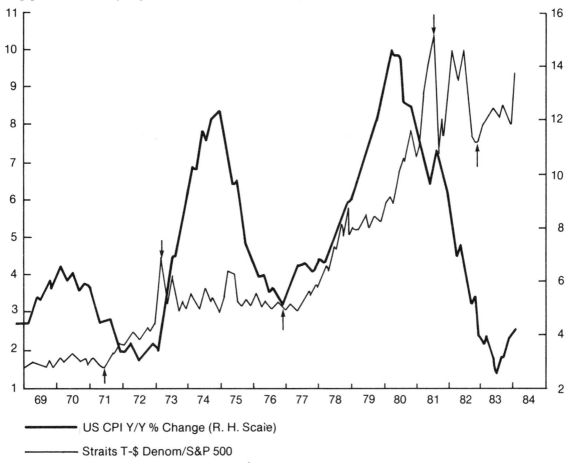

——— US CPI Y/Y % Change (R. H. Scale)

——— Straits T-$ Denom/S&P 500

As with Australia, the major part of the out-performance of the Singapore market against the rise in the U.S. market (Table 2) is captured by three time periods. The currency gain was much less significant, but still provided a certain amount of icing on the cake, at least in the last two rises. Given the close links between Singapore and Malaysia, we would expect a similar pattern to be evident in the relative currency-adjusted return for the Kuala Lumpur market.

Growing Non-Resource Economic Bases

These three markets do, indeed, provide the opportunity to increase the performance of a portfolio, but it would be a mistake to think of them as totally resource-based. All three countries have strong and growing industrial, commercial, and financial sectors, but as these sectors have much less volatility, the emphasis has tended to be on the more cyclical plays. To some extent, this may

TABLE 2. Singapore market

	4/71–2/73	12/76–6/81	10/82–2/84
Total relative change	261.9%	264.9%	40.5%
S&P Composite Index	12.8	24.9	14.0
Straits Times Index	305.4	290.8	55.5
S$/US$	−0.7	16.7	3.0
Duration of move (months)	22	66	16

FIGURE 3. Sector turnover as a percentage of total equity turnover

Australia		Singapore		Malaysia	
Year ended June 1983		Year ended December 1983			
Industrials	54.1	Industrials	62.0	Industrials	65.5
Mining	35.3	Financial	18.1	Financial	12.4
Oil and gas	10.6	Hotels	4.4	Hotels	1.9
		Properties	8.9	Properties	9.6
		Plantation	4.3	Tins	2.7
		Mining	2.3	Rubbers	5.1
				Oil palms	2.8
	100.0		100.0		100.0

now be less true in Australia, where most of the last increase in relative performance has been in the industrial stocks at a time of high capital inflows. This may have reflected hopes for short-term currency appreciation at a time when industrial activity was rising, however, while the outlook for commodities was unclear at best. We will, therefore, have to wait to see whether international investors will maintain this apparent new interest as commodities prices begin to firm.

To have a full perspective, it is important to note that each market under discussion does possess these other sectors and that in each market the value of the turn-over in the non-resource areas actually exceeds that in the resource based sectors (see Table 3). Industrials, for example, exceed 50 percent of turnover in all cases, and over 60 percent for Singapore and Malaysia. I would not be surprised if the ratio for Australia is much higher at present, given the rise in Australian commercial and industrial stocks over the last six months.

Factors Affecting the Timing Decision

In spite of the lower percentage of the value of resource stocks traded it is evident that there is a cyclical element, and this creates the potentially misleading impression that the decision on when to invest in these countries is relatively simple. There is a strong cyclical element in the resource cycle, for example, and this could be neatly tied in with fluctuations in world output. Figure 3 uses data generated by the OECD. It shows that six to nine months after demand accelerates, commodity prices begin to rise, and the resulting cycles are quite pronounced.

Not surprisingly, complications quickly arise. The top-down approach may rapidly give way to a bottom-up analysis. There are a number of

reasons for this, and at the risk of oversimplifying, I want to point out a few of them. First, although metal prices have fluctuated with cycles in world demand, the fluctuations have been generally very wide and have included periods of boom and bust. Timing on entering the markets is therefore vital, and of ever-increasing importance.

Second, although there is a rough correspondence between the cycles of different metals, such as at the peaks and troughs, the relationship with world demand is not close enough to affect each metal in the same way. The prices of the shares associated with those metals, which are very sensitive to expectations, quickly reflect the outlook for each metal separately.

Third, the nature of a world recovery will be reflected in the commodities which rise first. A consumer-led recovery, such as we witnessed in the United States last year, has resulted in a higher demand for cars. This should eventually translate into higher demand for natural rubber, which boosts Malaysia. Even this is oversimplistic. Competition from synthetic alternatives is increasing, and will also be reflected in final demand. In general, metals tend to boom only toward the end of a cycle.

Fourth, unseen circumstances may accentuate sharp fluctuations in commodity prices. The failure of this year's soybean crop and the U.S. PIK program immediately resulted in renewed demand for palm oil. This sharply raised prices and profits, and renewed buying in plantation stocks.

Finally, the share price for any given company will reflect the underlying resource portfolio. For example, one can point to the example of two Australian mining companies, CRA and MIM. The former recently showed considerable strength in outperforming the index, while the

FIGURE 3
Industrial production and non-oil commodity prices (percent deviation from phase-average trend)
Percent

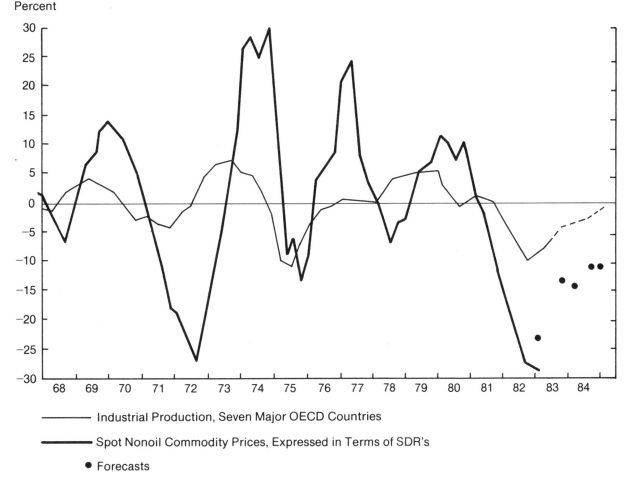

FIGURE 3
Industrial production and non-oil commodity prices (percent deviation from phase-average trend)
Percent

——— Industrial Production, Seven Major OECD Countries

▬▬▬ Spot Nonoil Commodity Prices, Expressed in Terms of SDR's

● Forecasts

latter did not. The poor performance of the latter company was primarily due to its higher exposure to copper, which has declined relative to the U.S. dollar. Similar considerations can be seen elsewhere in stocks in Malaysia and Singapore.

Valuation Considerations

In general, share prices tend to reflect the outlook for commodity prices. This makes valuation extremely difficult. The shares tend to have high P/E's and low dividend yields. These two measures are not very significant in Australia, since stocks are usually valued on a relative earnings/price basis. If a stock has no or low projected earnings, then it is generally valued on the basis of its sensitivity to commodity prices and its un-

derlying asset values. In practice, this differential is not so clear-cut, and the price probably reflects elements of both approaches. Even so, there are still many anomalies to the trend, both at the overall sector level and at the specific stock level.

The principal cause for these anomalies has been changes in the mineral composition within the individual companies' portfolios. To a large extent this has reflected the historical makeup of the portfolio of minerals, but it also reflects the degree of exposure to particular metals. In consequence there exists the kind of difference in performance illustrated by the CRA and MIM example.

A similar picture exists when investing in Southeast Asian plantation stocks. Such companies may have very high price/earnings ratios, and the outlook for commodity prices determines the share price. Although the fundamental basis for valuation may be an agricultural value per acre, the same anomalies as discussed earlier may arise, reflecting the composition of rubber, palm oil and/or cocoa, and even the maturity of the trees for any particular plantation. Two other factors have had an important influence upon the prices for these shares during the last ten years. The first of these is the "Malaysianization" of most of the major U.K. domiciled and controlled groups. The second is the property redevelopment potential for any acreage near urban areas.

Other Important Factors

There are also a few other points to be aware of when deciding to invest in Australia, Singapore, and Malaysia. A structural change is underway in the Australian stock market at the present time, with the removal of negotiated commissions. Unlike the advent of negotiated commissions in America—on "May Day"—the Australians have chosen the more appropriate date of April the first, or April Fool's Day, for their change.

The attitudes of the various governments toward foreign investment are also important. Generally, attitudes are sympathetic, particularly in Singapore and Malaysia. However, in Australia there is a 50 percent limit on overseas investors' holdings. This is likely to remain in view of the strength of the desire to retain local control of the development of the country's natural resources, a not unnatural feeling.

Foreign ownership of domestic Australian assets is a particularly sensitive area within the ruling Labor Party, but there is an equal awareness that if the country is to fully develop its resources, a steady inflow of investment will be needed. Thus, an uneasy truce lies between the two schools of thought, and the status quo is likely to remain, at least under the present government. Although the present Australian Prime Minister is liberalizing the financial markets, he may be prevented from moving too far by the left wing of his party. Equally, he has blunted the edge of some of the left-wing policies, particularly in regard to certain aspects of the uranium mining industry.

The existence of the 50 percent rule is unfortunately giving rise to an apparent move by Aus-

tralian companies to favor local institutions. Two recent examples of this attracted considerable criticism. Western Mining raised $123 million Australian dollars last year via a placing only with Australian institutions, and Ashton Mining conducted a similar exercise. While such developments are undesirable, given the vast potential of investing in Australia in general it should not prove too much of a barrier to us. The limitation on ownership does, however, accentuate the trading nature of the market.

Official government policy with regard to foreigners in Singapore and Malaysia is very positive. The cornerstone of this policy is the free movement of capital, interest, and dividends into and out of the two countries. In addition, the task of facilitating this free flow of capital has not been hampered by fears of currency weakness. Both currencies have shown strength against both the U.S. dollar and sterling since the Smithsonian Agreement in 1971.

However, as with Australia, some qualifications exist. First, in the so-called sensitive areas, such as banking, the percentage of foreign holdings in a particular stock is normally not allowed beyond a certain figure, usually 20 percent. A further practical but unlegislated barrier to ownership exists in both Malaysia and Singapore: Family-dominated companies predominate in those markets, and these have different definitions of control at high levels. This limits the free market and, for all practical purposes, limits foreign ownership of the shares concerned.

The second and more important issue is the Malaysian policy of increasing native Malay participation in the economy under the terms of the New Economic Policy. More stringent requirements on ownership will adversely affect those companies with major overseas connections and increase the relative attractiveness of companies with a Malaysian, if not Malay, identity.

No such issue as this faces investors in Singapore. However, close ties exist between the Singapore and Malaysian markets. Over the course of time, these markets are likely to drift apart as new listings now tend to be concentrated on one exchange or the other. But, today, the markets remain closely interlinked. To think of them otherwise is not to acknowledge the active two-way trade between them. It is important to realize, therefore, that although a stock may be registered on the Malaysian exchange, it can also be traded on the Singapore market, and with a few exceptions in certain plantation and tin companies, it is generally advisable to do so.

This brings me to my final point, which is the disclosure of information. In general, the availability of information is of a good and certainly improving standard, with most companies required to publish fully consolidated accounts. The major exceptions to this rule are the banks in Southeast Asia in general. Disclosure of information is based on the U.K. experience, with the spirit of self regulation being particularly noticeable in Australia. In Singapore and Malaysia, however, there are varying degrees of financial reporting in practice. There has recently been a healthy trend towards more meaningful financial disclosure, but at the present time the data base is still low in comparison with the United States. Nevertheless, some individual companies have taken the initiative to upgrade and broaden their financial reporting.

COMMODITY TRENDS KEY TO RESOURCE INVESTING

There should always be a place in a diversified international portfolio for investments in resource countries. It is important to realize that the fundamental factors are less relevant to resource-company share prices than is the outlook for commodity prices. Thus, for example, even though Australia itself has an extremely strong balance sheet, a rise in metal prices will quickly swamp the impact of other influences. This is a pity because each of the countries I have discussed possess strong industrial, commercial, and financial sectors, particularly Singapore. As long as the fluctuations in resource stocks are wide, in some cases presenting the opportunity for very substantial gains, international attention to these markets will continue to be focused predominantly on their resource stocks.

Global Investment Portfolios: Question and Answer Session

MODERATOR: I'd like to start by asking, first, if Japan is a long-term sell, and second, how portfolio managers can use Japanese brokers most effectively in their portfolio management process?

JEREMY PAULSON-ELLIS: To the first question, "Is Japan a long-term sell?" the answer must be "No" because Japan continues to produce a stream of products which are in demand worldwide and many of the companies that will produce these products over the next five years have still not been recognized in international terms. The problem in Japan is that the increasing pursuit of easy money, which was discussed today, is making it difficult to have the time to investigate, to look properly at particular shares before the share price has moved.

As to how to make the best use of the Japanese brokers, I think that's a very unfair one to throw at foreign brokers who have not been to Tokyo. But there is no doubt that they have done considerable work on the establishment of data bases. They unfortunately still have not realized that they have to take a longer-term look at what their plans are trying to achieve. If they can be persuaded to look at things on a longer-term basis, and with rather less emphasis on relationship financings and underwritings, I think that investors in France, the United States, and Europe are going to be much, much easier in their relationship to the Japanese experience.

BERTIE BOYD: There's no way you can call Japan a long-term sell! Fortunately for foreigners, going short in Japan is not difficult.

QUESTION: In a portfolio management context, does it make sense to have what you would call "core" positions in specific countries and in specific companies that you just buy and hold forever? Or, are all the countries up for grabs from a rotational point of view, and can all companies theoretically be rotated? Should you have core positions in your international portfolio?

IVAN PICTET: I certainly don't think you should have core positions in any particular portfolio.

But, in some markets you end up investing in many industries and companies which *are* "core holdings" in the sense that you might keep them longer than you would some others, particularly smaller growth companies or value-type stocks that are not expected to perform on a short-term basis.

QUESTION: Jeremy and Bertie, look on the flip side of that. Does it make sense, from a portfolio management point of view, to buy a series of very small, high-growth, less-liquid stocks and hold them, recognizing that you can't buy and sell them because of a lack of liquidity?

BERTIE BOYD: Yes.

QUESTION: For what portion of a portfolio would you adopt that strategy?

BERTIE BOYD: I think it has to be on a case-by-case basis. Everybody wants to have a bit of that kind of stock.

QUESTION: Is that like 5 percent of a portfolio, or would you go up to 15 percent, 20 percent, or 25 percent?

BERTIE BOYD: It would depend upon the nature of the whole portfolio and its size.

JEREMY PAULSON-ELLIS: More money has made by picking on the small- and medium-sized companies, all over the world. If you went down the list of winners in Japan over the last 20 years, you would certainly find that most of them, at one stage or another, had been run by extremely dominant single personalities, and they're not the great amorphous organizations you have in trading companies.

Therefore, what we see in Europe is the development of a range of products for institutional investors who actually have the funds to concentrate on smaller and medium-sized companies. The institution will have a subset of such holdings as an integral part of their overall Japanese portfolio.

QUESTION: Nobody has talked about Canadian stocks. For Americans, are they foreign stocks or are they domestic stocks? Ivan?

IVAN PICTET: I guess they are foreign stocks for Americans. I think they're unique. We consider them quite separately from the rest of the pack.

QUESTION: Earlier, the question was asked, "How do you expect to add value over the next three to five years in your portfolios?" If value added equalled 100 percent, how much would come each from currency, country, industry, and stock selection?

IVAN PICTET: The impression I get is, from a 5-year dollar standpoint, maybe something like 15 percent was required from currency. And maybe 15 percent to 20 percent for the company, and I go from numbers which start low. The other one, industry, must be the difference, 15 to 20 percent. Maybe industry should be 25 percent. Does that add up to 100 percent?

QUESTION: No; but with country at 40 percent it does. Mike?

MIKE DOBSON: I would say country—15 percent; industry—25 percent; and stock—40 percent.

QUESTION: Jeremy?

JEREMY PAULSON-ELLIS: We're all getting closer. Country—10 percent; currency—25 percent; industry—25 percent; stock—40 percent.

BERTIE BOYD: Well, I put currency at 5 percent because I don't know. Company—30 percent. We don't really ever work it on industry terms; that's about 5 percent, perhaps, and 70 percent stock.

QUESTION: Ivan, are you buying?

IVAN PICTET: No, I'm still not at 100. How about 15 percent for currency, 30 percent for the country, 35 percent for the industry, and 20 percent for the stock selection? Everyone should be happy.

QUESTION: On balance, stock selection is the heaviest, and country would be second.

When you come to country decisions, which three countries make the most sense for an American portfolio to *underweight* over the next three to five years, relative to the EAFE index? Mike?

MIKE DOBSON: I'd basically underweight in Europe. Most of the action is local.

IVAN PICTET: I think on a three-year, and maybe a five-year basis, I would underweight the United States at one point. I would overweight Europe, because I think the cycle is at a much earlier stage in Europe than it is either in the United States or in Japan. I've always thought that there were perhaps three years but two years is more likely; I would do that.

JEREMY PAULSON-ELLIS: Frankly, I find it difficult to pick out any markets, with the exception of United States and the United Kingdom, where you can take a judgment over a three-year period. After all, we've seen the volatility of some of these markets; I would pick out the United Kingdom.

BERTIE BOYD: I think I feel like Jeremy, if you're talking about estimating the possibilities five years from now.

QUESTION: If you're an investment manager based in the United States, or based in London or Europe, is it necessary to have an investment person actually located in the Far East in order to invest effectively in the Far East?

IVAN PICTET: We certainly think so. We have stockholders in Tokyo, and I think the input which we get from the stockholders has been very essential in our stock selection and in our understanding of the Japanese scene. The canned information sources in Japan don't come up with information that is very different, one from another, so I think the added value of an actual presence in Japan is clearly important.

MIKE DOBSON: We would agree with that. We make a split in terms of responsibility, and the decision as to how much to have in Japan is not made by our Japanese professionals in Tokyo. But we do allow them an enormous say in stock selection, particularly when it comes to smaller stocks.

MODERATOR: If you're all going to agree with that, I'm going to change the question just a little bit. Is it more appropriate to have the office in Tokyo or in Hong Kong?

JEREMY PAULSON-ELLIS: It depends. If you're spreading out your investments around the region, it makes no more sense to invest in Taiwan from Tokyo than to invest from Hong Kong. My preference would be to use Tokyo as the place to gather information quickly, to assess that information and to pass it on to fund managers wherever they might be.

BERTIE BOYD: I agree.